YO
GREATEST
ASSET

YOUR GREATEST ASSET

*Creative Vision and
Empowered Communication*

BY EARL NIGHTINGALE

© Copyright 2019 – Nightingale Conant Corporation

All rights reserved. This book is protected by the copyright laws of the United States of America. No part of this publication may be reproduced, stored in or introduced into a retrieval system, or transmitted, in any form or by any means (electronic, mechanical, photocopying, recording or otherwise), without the prior written permission of the publisher. For permissions requests, contact the publisher, addressed "Attention: Permissions Coordinator," at the address below.

Published and Distributed by

SOUND WISDOM
PO Box 310
Shippensburg, PA 17257-0310
717-530-2122

info@soundwisdom.com

www.soundwisdom.com

While efforts have been made to verify information contained in this publication, neither the author nor the publisher assumes any responsibility for errors, inaccuracies, or omissions. While this publication is chock-full of useful, practical information, it is not intended to be legal or accounting advice. All readers are advised to seek competent lawyers and accountants to follow laws and regulations that may apply to specific situations. The reader of this publication assumes responsibility for the use of the information. The author and publisher assume no responsibility or liability whatsoever on the behalf of the reader of this publication.

The scanning, uploading and distribution of this publication via the Internet or via any other means without the permission of the publisher is illegal and punishable by law. Please purchase only authorized editions and do not participate in or encourage piracy of copyrightable materials.

Originally part of Nightingale Success program.

Cover design by Eileen Rockwell

ISBN 13 TP: 978-1-64095-088-7

ISBN 13 eBook: 978-1-64095-089-4

For Worldwide Distribution, Printed in the U.S.A.

1 2 3 4 5 6 / 21 20 19

Table of Contents

	Preface 7
Chapter One	The Art of Relationships 11
Chapter Two	Strengthening Your Interpersonal Skills..... 29
Chapter Three	Building Effective Communication 39
Chapter Four	Improving Your Writing Skills 55
Chapter Five	Learning to Cultivate Your Creativity....... 69
Chapter Six	How to Apply Creativity to Problem-Solving......................... 89
Chapter Seven	How to Be a Master at Public Speaking..... 111
Chapter Eight	The Lasting Benefits of Good Service 139
	Earl Nightingale's Biography 161

Preface

THOSE WHO HAVE PULLED THEMSELVES out of a rut can attest to the importance of creative thinking to breaking through the monotony and finding fresh inspiration and motivation. For Earl Nightingale, an award-winning radio broadcaster and expert on success principles, creative thinking was the "secret sauce" to healthy relationships, excellence in leadership, success in business, and effectiveness in public speaking. Along with an open mindset and a worldview continually expanded through regular reading and study, Nightingale viewed problem-solving, decision-making, and goal achievement as necessary elements of creative thinking. But at the heart of all these elements is one crucial thing: attitude.

Nightingale says, "The way to keep from falling into the rut of routine and boredom is to remember the principle that anything can be improved upon, and it is the role of the human being to improve upon his life and his world. The thing to watch is your attitude toward your daily life." His broadcasts stress the integral role one's attitude toward his or her work and relationships plays in guaranteeing personal achievement and fulfillment. He repeatedly emphasizes the joy that comes from finding meaning in doing—meaning that derives from viewing one's pursuits as performed in service to others. According to Nightingale, there is one simple success equation: "your rewards will be determined by the way you do your job, multiplied by the number of people you serve."

In this volume, Nightingale asks his audience to imagine two bowls, one named "Rewards" and one named "Contributions." The problem, he notes, is that people concern themselves too much with adding to their "Rewards" bowl, but this inward focus does not lead to either wealth or happiness. Instead, we should concentrate on the bowl labeled "Contributions," and "life and basic economics will automatically take care of the rewards."

How, then, do we contribute to our families, our communities, and the world at large? Through the critical power of the imagination, exercised to build strong relationships, develop leaders, and create positive, sustainable change. With this in mind, *Your Greatest Asset* presents you with techniques and attitudes, which, if practiced regularly, will result in your living an even more creative, rewarding life.

The present volume derives from *The Essence of Success*, a collection of over one hundred of Nightingale's original audio scripts published in 1993 by Nightingale-Conant Corporation. As W. Clement Stone notes in his original foreword, these scripts "have been extracted from the firm's archives and gathered from the

Preface

private collections of many individuals who have contributed rare tapes and transcriptions to this tribute to one of the great motivational speakers and writers of this century."

Stone further explains: "Nightingale's radio colleague, Stephen D. King, whom Nightingale-Conant selected to narrate the audio version of *The Essence of Success*, recalls that the project began as a simple, heartfelt memorial to a broadcasting great, whose career spanned more than four decades. 'Earl's friends and colleagues began assembling a cross-section of his 40-year output. They took snippets of his tapes, found transcriptions of his early broadcasts, and delved into several hours of never-before-heard tapes of interviews he gave. Soon the project took on a life of its own,' King recalled. 'The more they collected, the more they wanted to collect. Radio old-timers, hearing about the project, contributed rare tapes and transcriptions.' What they assembled has gone on to become far more than a memorial."

Now, those messages in *The Essence of Success* pertaining to creative vision and interpersonal communication have been edited and re-collected in this transformative volume. The chapters selected will not only help you enhance your creative thinking strategies; they will also help you strengthen your communication skills in all realms of life. You will learn communication principles that run the gamut from how to become a better conversationalist (really, a better listener), to how to equip yourself to more effectively handle disagreements, to how to perfect your sales strategies, to how to form habits that are conducive to becoming a writer, to how to craft and deliver speeches that inspire confidence and engage audiences.

The power exists within you to actualize your dreams and use your gifts to better the world; this volume will help you cultivate the brainstorming, problem-solving, and communication skills necessary to do so.

Chapter One

The Art of Relationships

The Magic Marble

I WAS IN FARGO, NORTH CAROLINA, not long ago and ran across my old friend Fred Smith from Cincinnati. He told an interesting story about a friend of his who always holds a marble in his hand whenever he talks with someone. Fred had noticed that whenever he had talked to this man, he would reach into his pocket and out would come the marble, which he would hold all during the conversation. Fred asked him about it and told him it reminded him of Captain Queeg's ball bearings in Herman Wouk's *The Caine Mutiny*.

His friend laughed and said, "This is my magic marble, Fred. Years ago, I had a hard time getting along with people. I knew a great many people but actually had very few friends. One day, I was talking with one of these friends when I noticed his attention wander. I was talking, but he was looking out of the window, his thoughts a million miles away. Later, I got to thinking about it and made a very embarrassing discovery. I realized that I had been talking about myself. I realized at the same time that I always talked about myself. Conversations with others were really nothing more than opportunities to talk about what I was doing, what I thought about a subject. When others were talking, I wasn't thinking much about what they were saying, I was reloading, getting ready to tell them all about myself. And it dawned on me why I had so few friends: I wasn't being a friend. I wasn't interested in what was happening to others and what they thought at all. So I made up my mind to change. I made up my mind to become interested in others, to let them do the talking, to steer the conversation back to them and their ideas. But it's difficult to break a habit of years, so I dropped into a five and dime and bought this marble. I call the marble 'Importance,' and I make sure it's always on the side of the other person.

"Whenever someone talks to me, I hold the marble in my hand and make sure it's on the side of the other person. I've never had a problem with people since. That little marble has made hundreds of friends for me. It's also taught me to quit thinking about myself all the time," he went on to say. "And I've found myself becoming genuinely interested in others. When that happens, you make friends in a hurry."

Well, that's the story of the magic marble. When I heard it, it made me think long and soberly about my own conduct in conversations. I asked myself if I'd been tossing the ball to the other person or trying to hog the conversation with regard to my own interests. I wasn't sure, so I started making sure.

The thing to remember here is that other people are far more interested in themselves than they are in you. You accomplish nothing talking about yourself, but you accomplish a great deal by showing interest in what the other person is saying and doing. You make him feel that he or she is important in your eyes, and whenever you do this well, you might call it "instant friendships." It works like a charm every time.

So ask yourself the same question. How are you in the magic marble department? When others are talking, do you find interest in what they're saying, or are you just waiting for your chance to jump in and dominate the conversation?

We'd all do well, I suppose, if we'd buy ourselves a little magic marble and hold it in our hands each time we enter into a conversation with someone. The marble's name, remember, is Importance, and the idea is to make certain it's with the other person.

On Caring

I WAS READING STUDS TERKEL'S BOOK *Working,* and one of the interviews is with a young steel worker. He hates his work; he's tired and bruised and burned all the time, but he's willing to put up with it because of his kids. He sees his kids getting good educations, even though they're still quite small, and not having to work and live the way he does. As the steel worker says, "This is why I work.

Every time I see a young guy walk by with a shirt and tie and dressed up real sharp, I'm lookin' at my kid, you know? That's it." The young steel worker will put up with a job he hates, for all those tedious years, because he thinks he can help his kids do better, not make the mistakes he's made, not find themselves in the trap he's in.

I received a letter from a listener recommending the book *On Caring* by Milton Mayeroff. Mayeroff writes, "Man finds himself by finding his place, and he finds his place by finding appropriate others that need his care and that he needs to care for. Through caring and being cared for, we experience ourselves as a part of nature; we are closest to a person or an idea when we help it grow." That's beautiful.

And he says, "In the sense in which a man can ever be said to be at home in the world, he is at home not through dominating or explaining or appreciating, but through caring and being cared for."

And I suspect that that's what keeps millions at work they don't particularly like, putting in year after year, with not much light at the end of the tunnel. It's because there's someone else, someone to care for—someone to hope and plan and dream for. We find our place "by finding appropriate others that need [our] care and that [we need] to care for. Through caring and being cared for, we experience ourselves as a part of nature; we are closest to a person or an idea when we help it grow."

People and/or ideas can give meaning to our lives. If we happen to lack one, we can make do with the other. If we have both, we're most fortunate. It's when both are absent from our lives that we become alienated and depressed and feel there's no reason for living.

Parents by the thousands have spent most of their years in the most menial, back-breaking, discouraging kind of work to make certain their kids are properly fed and clothed and sent to school. Like the steel worker in our example, the well-being of their children fills their minds and their daily lives, and they'll put up with anything and go to work so sick that they can hardly drag themselves out of bed.

And when we see people hurrying home in the evening, we can understand that they're heading for what gives meaning to their lives—someone to care for and someone who cares for them. They may not put it into words or even fully understand it, but that's what coming home is all about. And that's what keeps them going week after week, year after year—others who need their care and whom they need to care for.

Friendships and Selflessness

AS ROBERT LOUIS STEVENSON WROTE, "There is no duty we so much underrate as the duty of being happy." Did you ever think much about that? There is much truth in this—how much we can barely guess from the many people we all know who live by cursing their jobs, their wives, their husbands, their kids, the weather, and the politicians and the government. How many people drink too much only to forget their lives that could make them happy—should make them happy—or lives they should change if they don't! Most of us are luckier than we know and have much to celebrate.

But happiness and joyful celebrations are inconceivable without friends, and it is awful to imagine the loneliness of otherwise fortunate people who have no friends anywhere. Their plight should give us pause, because most of us find that, through neglect, the number of our own friends has declined with the years. So when a person reaches age fifty, the condition of his friendships may need more attention than it did long ago.

Aristotle discovered three kinds of friendships worthy of the name. The first is based on utility; an example would be a friendship between people who do business together. The second has its roots in a quest for pleasure; it can be seen in the case of friendship between amusing or quick-witted persons. The third is the best; in it each friend seeks nothing beyond the company and the happiness of the other. Most poets who write about friendships mean only Aristotle's third and best kind, while in everyday speech, we commonly refer to all three types as if they were the same.

Selflessness is the rule in the best of friendships. What benefits my friend benefits me; what benefits me benefits him. This is so, not because we share our worldly goods with each other (we don't), but because, being true friends, we take pleasure in each other's good fortune.

It's true that people who are friends in the deepest sense do favors for each other, but these favors, whether large or small, are an incidental part of the friendship and are not essential to its prosperity. A friend is an extension of oneself. It is pleasant to visit with a friend; it is even pleasant simply to know that he exists. Somehow that knowledge improves the world immensely, making it at once a warmer and more secure place in which to live.

Perhaps Walt Whitman put it best in two lines. He wrote, "Stranger, if you, passing, meet me, and desire to speak to me, why should you not speak to me? And why should I not speak to you?"

Friendships and Change

Our best and most lasting friends are those who think along the same lines, believe in the same things, and who constantly challenge us to move ahead with them into increasing mental and emotional maturity.

HERBERT BAYARD SWOPE ONCE SAID, in replying to the tributes paid to him at a testimonial dinner, "I cannot give you the formula for success, but I can give you the formula for failure: try to please everybody."

One of the mistakes frequently made by most people is to believe you should keep all of your friends all of your life. It not only cannot be done; it shouldn't be done.

H. L. Mencken once said, "One of the most mawkish of human delusions is the notion that friendship be lifelong. The fact is that a man of resilient mind outwears his friendship just as certainly as he outwears his love affairs and his politics. They become threadbare, and every act and attitude that they involve becomes an act of hypocrisy."

As usual, Mencken put it as bluntly as the English language will possibly allow, but again, as usual, he was right.

If you believe otherwise, you believe that a girl or boy should marry the first person he or she likes or has a crush on, or that we should still be going around with the same group we went to school with.

Mencken went on to say, "A prudent man, remembering that life is short, examines his friendships critically now and then. A few he retains, but the majority he tries to forget."

And on the same subject, George Bernard Shaw once said, "The only man who behaves sensibly is my tailor; he takes my measurements anew each time he sees me, whilst all the rest go on with their old measurements and expect them to fit me."

Living means changing, and changing means (or at least should mean) forming new friendships and discarding some of those we outwear. No two people mature at the same rate; some move ahead faster than others, and it is just ridiculous to try to retain all of our old friendships.

Yet often people will feel guilty about outgrowing a friendship; they'll think they're becoming snobbish or too fussy about their friends, when actually it's perfectly natural.

I do think that when we get older, we form stronger and more lasting friendships than when we were young, changing, and moving around a lot. Our best and most lasting friends are those who think along the same lines, believe in the same things, and who constantly challenge us to move ahead with them into increasing mental and emotional maturity. They are the friends we enjoy spending an evening with, with a lot of good conversation over dinner and, maybe, far into the night.

Again regarding friendship, Mencken said, "A prudent man remembering that life is short examines his friendships critically now and then. A few he retains, but the majority he tries to forget."

Have I Told You Lately?

I RECEIVED A PAPERBACK BOOK from some friends of mine. The book is titled *A Touch of Wonder* by Arthur Gordon.

I opened the book at random to a chapter on "The Gift of Caring." In it, Gordon tells about going through the attic of an old house in Georgia in which the family had lived for a century and a half. The attic was filled with the junk of generations, but he found something of value all the same. Arthur Gordon said he "found it in the letters, a whole trunkful of them." He wrote, "Most of them were written in faded ink and were grimy with the dust of decades. We'd stand there in the shuttered gloom, ankle-deep in mismatched spurs and andirons, in tarnished epaulets, and scraps of torn lace or faded brocade, and read a paragraph or two. And it was like listening to voices, faint and far away, echoing down the corridor of time."

What struck him most about the letters was the frankness of the writers writing in an age when cynicism didn't demand that we withhold our tenderest sentiments, a time when people said what was in their hearts. To quote him: "In a hundred different ways, they spoke of their love and admiration for one another, and you could feel their sincerity warm on the brittle paper:

"'You don't know how much your visit meant to each of us! When you left, I felt as if the sun had stopped shining.'

"'The courage with which you are facing your difficulties is an inspiration to all of us. We haven't the slightest doubt that in the end you will triumph over all of them.'"

But this is the one that impressed me most and which is no doubt spoken all too seldom in far too many families:

"'Have I told you lately what a wonderful person you are? Never forget how much your friends and family love and admire you.'

"How wonderful you are!" Arthur Gordon writes, "That was the steady refrain, and it made me stop and think. In each of these people, no doubt, there had been much that could have been criticized. But when you remembered the times they had lived through—the way that ended for them in poverty and bitterness and defeat, the terrifying epidemics of yellow fever—it was impossible to escape the conclusion that the writers of these letters were stronger than we are—that they faced greater tests with greater fortitude. And where did they get their strength? That answer lay in my dusty hands. They got it from one another."

They got it from the same place our kids need it—from us and from their friends, the same place from which we need to hear it and feel it.

When was the last time you said those words to the people who needed it? "Have I told you lately what a wonderful person you are?

Never forget how much your friends and family love and admire you."

Home Is Like a Lifeboat

HERE'S A LITTLE EXERCISE in imagination for you. Let's say you were shipwrecked and found yourself in a small boat, or on a small island, with a handful of other survivors. How long do you think you would all get along well together? How long would it be before different personalities would begin to chafe and wear thin?

A family is, in many ways, like a small group that has been marooned. The members of the family are stuck with each other. Every morning, every night, and on weekends the little group must get along and live together. No two of the members are alike; each has a completely different personality, different likes and dislikes. Each has problems that he or she considers to be important; each sees the world and life from his or her own unique viewpoint and with his or her interests in mind.

Yet they must live close together, in the most intimate of relationships, for year after year after year. This can give you an idea why the happy, loving family is about as rare as twenty-five-carat diamonds. It's also why, in even the best managed and usually happy homes, there are times when visiting these homes is like jumping into a river full of piranhas. Someone reaches the breaking point when someone else goes a little too far and suddenly war is declared.

It is believed that much of the discord in the average household could be avoided if more people realized that they're in this lifeboat, or small island predicament—that is, if they understood a little better that human beings—any and all human beings—have trouble getting along when they're jammed into close quarters for an extended period of time.

The man and his wife and the kids who are old enough to be reached with this idea need to understand that the problem does not necessarily lie with Charlie, or Joan, or little Willie, or whatever their names are. They need to understand that the same problem would exist no matter who on earth they happened to live with. Everyone has faults. Changing husbands or wives and raising new kids is nothing more than changing one set of problems for another.

I think the lifeboat analogy is particularly apt because a home is, in many respects, like a lifeboat; it's the way to life and survival. But the problems are built in and should be discussed so that every member of the family makes a constant conscious effort to contribute to the well-being and success of so precarious a journey. Understanding the problem could keep someone from being pitched overboard.

When all the people in a boat are pulling together, each one giving of himself for the good of all, the odds are good that they'll have a safe journey.

YOUR GREATEST ASSET

When was the last time you got angry at your spouse? At your children? At your parents?

Have you ever tried to consciously accept a family member for who they are?

Try acknowledging others' faults as a unique part of their total personality, and forgive them for being human.

YOUR GREATEST ASSET

How's Your Marriage Today?

WELL, HOW'S MARRIED LIFE these days? You know, during the terrible purges in Russia, a woman would discover one evening that her husband wasn't coming home. Instead, he was being sent to a slave-labor camp in Siberia for ten or twenty years—probably forever, because of the conditions at the camps. One day he went off to work as usual, and that was the last time she saw him—unless she joined the crowds at the railway station and happened to catch a glimpse of him as he was loaded into the cattle cars with the other prisoners.

It's a terrible thought, isn't it? And what were his thoughts of her as he began his lonely pilgrimage? Probably both of them thought only of the fine qualities of the other one, and no doubt they were filled with a sudden, poignant love for each other.

They very probably tortured themselves by thinking of all the things they might have said or done but failed to do. (Dostoyevsky has given us some unforgettable glimpses into this sort of thing.)

Well, how's your marriage today? Has it quietly fashioned itself into a smooth, well-worn rut? Do you take your marriage and each other for granted? Or do you, like the few wise ones, keep finding new and interesting ways of renewing your awareness of, and affection for, each other—ways that keep the marriage young and interesting?

I'll stick my neck out and generalize that the great majority of marriages are about as interesting as the great majority of people. A person will give to his marriage the same attitude that he habitually gives to his life. If his life is filled with interest, so is his marriage. If his life is not interesting, he is a fool. And fools don't build interesting marriages.

Now, let me modify all this by saying that a daily routine can easily form a trap into which just about anyone can fall. The way to keep from falling into the rut of routine and boredom is to remember the principle that anything can be improved upon, and it is the role of the human being to improve upon his life and his world.

Think of the great and sudden leap forward our national industry would experience if, on some morning, every working person went to work with the idea of finding some way to improve his job and his attitude toward those with whom he works—and, at the same time, took the same attitude toward his marriage. Just as the sudden influx of new ideas would bring freshness and new power to his job, the same thing would happen at home. The dullness, the ennui, the routine would vanish. The marriage would be renewed, revitalized.

The thing to watch is your attitude toward your daily life. If you are the kind of person who makes his daily life interesting, who is constantly on the alert for new ways of enhancing and putting new challenges into things, then chances are you have an interesting and enjoyable marriage. If not, you might give some thoughts to it. And remember the Siberia story, and do and say the things you should now so that you will never be filled with remorse if anything should happen.

And perhaps I should end this with a comment by Balzac. He wrote, "Love, according to our contemporary poets, is a privilege which two beings confer upon one another, whereby they may mutually cause one another much sorrow over absolutely nothing."

Growing Up Demands Courtesy

If there's a keyword to successful child raising, I rather imagine it's the same word found as the cornerstone of a successful marriage—and the word is courtesy. It's showing those we love and for whom we are entirely responsible the common courtesy and respect we show to total strangers and our neighbors.

I REMEMBER HEARING an angry father shout at his twelve-year-old son, "Why don't you grow up?"

There was a sudden silence in the room, and then the boy, his face working to control his tears, quietly said, "That's what I'm trying to do."

That's what all young people are trying to do, and it's not an easy job. As adults, we tend to be impatient with others who cannot do well and quickly learn something that took us perhaps years to learn if, indeed, we've completely learned it ourselves.

To the skilled in anything, the fumbling, awkward attempts of the novice often seem ludicrous or exasperating, if not totally incomprehensible. "No, no," we say, "that's not the way to do it!" And we charge in to take over. In doing so, we add humiliation and self-consciousness to the beginner's feelings of inadequacy.

And as a person will do when he is humiliated, when he is shown himself as an inept, bungling fool, he will begin to dislike us. And it can change to hate. There will begin building within him a burning, inarticulate lump of pure, raw, primitive, dangerous hate. And each time we tell him how inadequate he is, with loving phrases such as "Won't you ever learn?" or "You're impossible" or "You can't do anything right" or "Why don't you grow up?" we feed a little additional fuel to the furnace.

If someone talked to us that way, we'd punch him in the nose. But a youngster can't punch his parent in the nose, as much as he'd love to at times, so that fire just builds within him. He reacts to the parent who treats him in this manner just exactly as you or I would: he doesn't like him, and eventually he hates him.

He doesn't want to. He's terribly disappointed in the parent as well as in himself. He's torn by the wish to love, the need to love, and the hate he feels—the ambivalence.

This is the kind of tumultuous inner battle that an adult finds most difficult to handle and resolve. In a child or a very young person, when everything in life looms so much bigger, so much more final, more terrible, it takes on catastrophic proportions.

Later, when the young person has grown into adulthood and hopefully some degree of maturity, he and his parent, or parents, may become friends again. He may even make exactly the same dumb mistakes with his kids.

But it's a costly shame that we look upon our children, so often, differently from the way we look at other people. And not all parents do. Some parents treat their youngsters with courtesy, respect, and love, and, at the same time, lay down firm guidelines and rules of conduct.

Being a good parent must surely be one of the world's most difficult jobs, exceeded in difficulty only by the process of growing up itself. It's a job for which most of us had no training, with little more than the resolution to try to do a better job than our parents did with us.

But if there's a keyword to successful child raising, I rather imagine it's the same word found as the cornerstone of a successful marriage—and the word is *courtesy*. It's showing those we love and for whom we are entirely responsible the common courtesy and respect we show to total strangers and our neighbors.

Living in such close and constant proximity makes this difficult perhaps, but no less necessary.

Chapter Two

Strengthening Your Interpersonal Skills

Earning the Right to Be Wrong

THE MOST IMPORTANT SUBJECT a person can learn, I suppose, is how to get along well with others. And one of the most important rules in mastering this most difficult subject is knowing when to be wrong, even if you're right.

There is no more exasperating human being on earth than the one who insists upon being right all the time. This is the person who feels that to be wrong, or not know the answer to something, means, at least for the moment, the end of the world.

I was spending some time with friends in Arizona some time back. One night we were going someplace in the car and my friend's father was driving. We came to the road where we should turn, and seeing that our driver was going to go blithely by the turnoff, both of us suddenly told him that this was where we should turn. It caught him by surprise; he suddenly braked the car and managed to make the turn, not easily, and as he did so, he said, "I know. I know this is where we turn."

Now, the fact of the matter was that he had not known. It was apparent to everyone in the car, but he was just one of those people who simply cannot admit there's something they don't know. My friend winked at me. But later he said, "I wish Dad would admit once in a while that there are things in the world he doesn't know; I wish he would admit he can be wrong like the rest of us."

How much better it would have been, how much more human a person he would have been, if he simply smiled and said, "Thanks for telling me. I'd have gone right on by." This would not have diminished him one whit in our eyes; it's perfectly human to make mistakes or not know something. But his actual response—his obvious cover-up and attempt to make us think he had known about the turnoff—did diminish him in our eyes. It caused us to feel sorry for him, and it pushed him a little ways out of our circle of companionship.

The worker who insists upon always being right is disliked by his associates, his subordinates, and his boss. He'd be much better off to make it a point to be wrong once in a while and say so.

The smart manager and executive knows the value of being wrong occasionally, even when he's right. There will come times when he's going to have to insist upon being right, so he can afford to graciously give in when it comes to small and unimportant matters.

In *Nation's Business*, it is suggested that before you tell a subordinate that you're right and he's wrong, ask yourself exactly what's to be gained and what is to be lost by deflating him. It might be a small matter to you; it could mean a complete loss of face to him.

Giving in is also better for your health. Dr. George Stevenson of the National Association for Mental Health says, "Even if you're dead right, it's easier on your system to give in once in a while. And," he added, "if you yield, you'll usually find that others will, too."

Try it with the members of your family. You'll be amazed at how it cuts down on the number of arguments and the way you'll find other people suddenly saying to you, "No, I'm wrong and you're right."

It's a whole lot better to say you're wrong, even when you know you're right, and get along well with others than it is to insist you're right at the expense of being disliked.

The Miserable Moth-Eaten Grudge

In my opinion, there are two main points here to keep in mind: The first is that disagreements with those we love are inevitable. They will—they must—happen from time to time. The second is that when they do happen, limit what you say to a minimum. Then shut up and wait.

THERE ARE THOUSANDS OF FAMILIES in the country that are host to running feuds of various kinds, all because they're too dumb to realize that occasional fights are as much a part of being related as consanguinity—as descending from the same ancestors. But you'd be surprised at the number of people who don't understand about disagreements with people we're supposed to like and get along with. Just as occasional hot disagreements are normal, so is the passing of the disagreement...if you'll let it pass.

I know of a case where a young woman will not speak or communicate in any way with her parents or her sister because of a disagreement and the resulting verbal battle. And this is a common kind of thing. Somebody does something wrong or says the wrong thing and people act as though it's the end of the world. Let a day or two go by, or maybe a few hours, and with willingness to become friends again it will all blow over and you'll be laughing about it.

But people will cling to their miserable, moth-eaten little grudge for dear life, feeding it, keeping it alive despite all its attempts to die, whipping it back into life and maintaining their misery and the misery of others at all costs. These people have the depth and breadth of a teaspoonful of tepid canal water and the sense of humor of a hungry shrew; the lines of bitterness become etched about their mouths. They are people who are filled with themselves—whose horizons are so close that their hair hangs over them. And you'll find a sprinkling of them on every block, I suppose. There is little or no light and sunshine in their lives.

In my opinion, there are two main points here to keep in mind: The first is that disagreements with those we love are inevitable. They will—they must—happen from time to time. The second is that when they do happen, limit what you say to a minimum. Then shut up and wait. That is, state your case as clearly as you can and then wait for a little time to blow the disagreement away, as it will every time. No matter how serious the disagreement may have seemed at the time, a day or so later it will have softened, blurred, and perhaps disappeared entirely. Quite often, people feuding with each other have long forgotten the cause of the original dispute.

The mature, serene person has outgrown petty feuds and realizes that his position is as vulnerable to being wrong as the other person's. And sometimes a difference of opinion can have both disputants in the right but with different ideas. Let the other person have the right to his opinion.

There are times in most of our lives when, at that moment, we would be delighted to agree never to see that particular person again as long as we live. An hour or two, or a day or so later, we'll feel differently about it. The trick is not to go too far—not to commit yourself to a course of action that makes reconciliation difficult, embarrassing, or awkward. And the answer is usually silence. You won't make many mistakes with your mouth shut.

The Qualities of a Leader

A person in authority is not necessarily a saint, an artist, a philosopher, or a hero, but he respects truth, appreciates what is beautiful, knows how to behave himself, and is courageous in meeting his obligations.

HE WILL HAVE INTELLECTUAL CURIOSITY and will be always learning. He is tolerant, liberal and unshockable. If he is not always affable and urbane, he at least is never truculent or overbearing. He will be a cultured, broadminded scholar who lives according to the spirit of reasonableness."

That's a definition of a leader. How did you qualify? A leader is a person in authority, such as a parent or boss of any sort. A Hindu proverb says, "There is nothing noble in feeling superior to some other person. The true nobility is in being superior to your previous self." Those who have shown that they can lead their own lives effectively are best fitted to accept responsibility and authority. The true function of leadership is to bring out the best efforts of others, and people most willingly pay heed to those whom they consider most able to direct.

The best leaders are almost always those who do not seek leadership but who have demonstrated in their own lives, in their work and attitude, that they should lead. The desire for power was to the Greeks and the early Christian church a reason for not giving it. Plato's rulers were to be given absolute power only upon the condition that they did not want it, and a man appointed to the episcopacy in the church was required to say, "I do not want to be a bishop."

The problem is that social and industrial progress are impossible where there is no one in authority. There must be someone in control of an operation if anything useful or distinguished is to get done.

"Authority" means having the power to judge and act, to issue instructions and enforce obedience. These are qualities that are not found in committees but in strong personalities. Yet you want a person who does not deliberately seek power.

The animal kingdom is studded with evidence of creatures in authority, from the pecking order of the birds to the stamping ground of the buffalo. Every mass human activity needs and has an elite group of qualified persons exercising the major share of authority. The excuse for an elite is that it takes the lead and accepts accountability.

For its very existence, human society demands order. No way has been found in modern civilization of producing order without allocating a degree of authority. This is clearly evident in the armed forces, in education, in law enforcement, in business, in government, and in sports. An umpire is a person in authority, and many a player has been thrown out of a game because he failed to recognize that—managers, too.

The leader is the person who acts when the situation requires action. The masses do not accomplish much in history; they follow the lead of people of purpose, able to plan, fit to administer. They make the difference. And we never have enough of the right kind.

YOUR GREATEST ASSET

Do you have the qualities of leadership?

Can you bring out the best qualities in others?

Have you demonstrated that you can lead your life effectively?

Do you have the power to judge and act, issue instructions and enforce obedience?

Do you act when a situation requires action?

Finding Hidden Reservoirs of Potential

THE GREAT PEOPLE OF THE WORLD, whether they're teachers, parents, business executives, or leaders in any field, know that where human beings are concerned, there is always much more there than meets the eye. An excellent example of this can be found in a story told by George Marek, formerly vice president of RCA Victor Records. The story was printed some years back in the *Reader's Digest*.

It seems that when the NBC Symphony was about to be formed, David Sarnoff, chairman of the board of NBC, gave one directive: "Do not hire away any players from existing orchestras because that would only weaken other orchestras." The people in charge, headed by Artur Rodziński, himself a fine conductor, managed to get together a superb orchestra—all except the first clarinetist.

When the great maestro Toscanini was about to arrive from Italy to take over the orchestra, Sarnoff was asked how the problem should be handled. Should Toscanini be left to find out for himself? Should they tell him frankly? Sarnoff said, "Let's tell him." His associates said, "You tell him." Accordingly, a delegation went down to meet the boat.

In his stateroom, Toscanini greeted Sarnoff and said, "That's a fine orchestra you got together—very fine, all except the first clarinetist." Sarnoff was taken aback. And he asked, "Maestro, how did you find out?" Toscanini said, "I have been listening on a little shortwave radio I had in Milan, and I could tell." Yes, he could hear it on a little radio in Milan.

Toscanini then said, "Take me to the studios." There the orchestra was rehearsing, and a special dressing room was waiting for him. He sent for the clarinetist, who arrived in such a state of mind as you can easily imagine. Toscanini said to him, "You are a good clarinet player, but there are certain things that you do wrong." Then he began to work with him. The upshot was that the clarinetist stayed with the orchestra for seventeen years and became one of the world's best.

All too often we're prone to look upon people as they are instead of in light of what they might be—what they can be. Instead of firing or giving up on a person, maybe a little patience, encouragement, and lots of training can help him evolve into the person you're looking for.

I remember hearing a story concerning Dr. Robert Hutchins when he was president of the University of Chicago. They were having a discussion of adult education, I think it was, and someone made the comment that you can't teach old dogs new tricks, to which Dr. Hutchins responded, "Human beings are not dogs and education is not a bag of tricks."

Frequently we expect too much too soon of a person or overlook problems that may be standing in the way. Parents are quite often amazed to discover their children emerging into intelligent, responsible adults quite capable of living successfully in the world. It just took some time on everyone's part.

As the experts have pointed out, there exists in each of us deep reservations of ability, even genius, which we habitually fail to use. It often takes knowledge, care, and time to bring ability to the surface.

Chapter Three

BUILDING EFFECTIVE COMMUNICATION

Sharpening Your Listening Skill

THE EXPERTS ESTIMATE that most of us spend about 70 percent of our waking hours in some form of verbal communication. It breaks down this way: 9 percent of our time is spent writing; 16 percent is spent reading; 30 percent is devoted to talking; and 45 percent—almost half the time we're awake—is spent listening. So you see, it really is a good idea to know how to listen—how to get more good out of what we hear.

The first suggestion is to recognize the importance of skillful listening. If we don't realize it's worthwhile to hear more of what people say to us, there's no reason to bother improving this creative power.

Second, we should pay attention. Now, while this may seem too obvious even to mention, it's surprising how many people try to fake their attention. And it's awfully embarrassing when they get caught at it. While listening to someone, we should look at them—squarely in the eye is always best—and give them the attention and respect we appreciate so much when we're speaking. If, instead of listening to a person, we're trying to figure out what we're going to say next, we can't possibly keep up with what that person is telling us.

Third, we should keep alert to the speaker's gestures and facial expressions. Empathy is one of the outstanding marks of a good listener. None of us likes to talk with someone who persists in wearing a deadpan expression, so try smiling occasionally and nodding in agreement. This tactic is just as positive as a yawn is negative.

Fourth, we ought never to rule out any topic of discussion as totally uninteresting. Creative people are always on the lookout for new and different information. While we may rightly classify some topics as "drivel"—gossip being one candidate for this list—it's wise to be sure the subject is not worthwhile before tuning it out. Keep your mind open to new ideas. They're all around you, and many of them will come by way of the spoken word.

Fifth, avoid prejudging the speaker—pay attention to what he's saying rather than the way he says it. Closed-mindedness and jumping to conclusions might well come under this heading. An excellent example of prejudging and missing the point entirely occurred about a hundred years ago when a brilliant speech by Edward Everett, which lasted some two hours, was followed by another, delivered by a gangling giant of a man who spoke only ten sentences. When he finished, there was a smattering of polite applause. But what that battlefield crowd had just listened to and not heard—had dismissed completely because of the second speaker's brevity and awkward manner—was the Gettysburg Address, delivered by Abraham Lincoln.

Here's the sixth suggestion for increasing your listening power: take brief notes while listening. When these are reviewed later, they jog the memory and bring back to mind the speaker's main points. Here again you can see the value of keeping a pencil handy.

Seventh, look for the speaker's purpose—what he's trying to get across. Search for his main ideas, and distinguish facts from fiction.

Eighth, we should beware of our "emotional deaf spots" that have a tendency to turn off our hearing. These are often words or ideas that strike us the wrong way. If we know of such "deaf spots," we can begin removing them by defining the word or idea that's bothering us, analyzing the matter completely, and discussing it with a good friend or member of the family. Once we realize that a situation like this exists, it's relatively simple to cure it.

Ninth, be observant—listen for areas of mutual interest—and resist distractions. You know, while our minds can think at a speed of 500 words per minute, we normally talk at about 125 words a minute. There are three things we can do to keep our rapid thinking concentrated on what's being said: First, weigh and evaluate the material as we listen; think more about it. Second, think ahead; anticipate the next area to be covered. And third, think back; recapitulate. A quick recap helps our memory. It greatly increases our retention of what we've been told.

Tenth and finally, discuss the skill of listening with your business associates, your friends, and your family. By talking about things that are important to us, we reinforce and simplify our own understanding. Good listening pays high dividends—in business, socially, and in our personal lives.

The Art of Listening

Listening really is the key to good conversation. You can't learn much with your own mouth open.

THE LATE BENNETT CERF told of a college professor, much admired in his field, who would often invite his more promising students to his home for informal get togethers. On one occasion, an eager sophomore asked, "Professor, what's the secret of the art of good conversation?"

The professor held up an admonishing finger and said, "Listen."

After a long minute had passed, the sophomore said, "Well, I'm listening." And the professor said, "That is the secret."

It is also something that we would do well to check ourselves on from time to time. What brought this story to mind was a luncheon I recently suffered through in the company of a person who obviously had never taken the time to learn the secret of the art of conversation. I am sure you know the type. He can be recognized by his rapidly moving mouth, from which issues little or nothing of value. He seems to feel there is something wrong with silence and reflection.

Someone else has said that good conversation is like a tennis match in which the subject of conversation is lobbed back and forth, with everyone participating. But with those who have not learned this valuable art, you are more like a spectator at a golf match, simply standing by while someone keeps hitting his own ball.

These are times when you would like to have a tape recorder and a hidden microphone so you could send the conversation-dominator a recording of his one-way diatribe. Then he could hear himself riding roughshod over others, curtly dismissing their comments, and churning back into his own stream of sound like a hippopotamus in a mill pond.

Listening really is the key to good conversation. You can't learn much with your own mouth open. Whatever you say has to be something you already know—unless you are guessing or, worse still, faking, in which case you are riding for an embarrassing fall.

The most embarrassing moments I can recall have been times when I was talking when I should have been listening. So every once in a while, I remind myself to be a good listener. Then, when it is my turn to add something to the general conversation, perhaps I can add something of value or interest.

It's not an easy thing to do, especially when the conversation turns to a subject on which you have a strong opinion. There is a great temptation to jump in with both feet, flailing arms and working jaw, submerging the entire room in one's great wisdom. But if one will summon the self-control and resist the urge, one can then parcel out his familiarity with the subject in small amounts. This permits others to share the topic. A person just might, through this method, manage to sound relatively intelligent all evening—or even learn something.

And if you run across a conversation hog, don't try to compete. If he runs down, which isn't likely, toss him another subject. You will find he is an expert on everything under the sun, and while he is talking, you can be thinking constructively of something else—and enjoying your lunch.

On Conversation

ONCE UPON A TIME there was an old man who was given to talking to himself. One sunny morning, he was engaged in this practice and an old friend of his said, "Charlie, you're talking to yourself again."

"I know it," Charlie replied. "Well, why do you do it?" his friend asked. "For two very good reasons," the old man answered. "The first reason is because I enjoy talking to an intelligent man. And the second is that I enjoy hearing an intelligent man talk."

This is a story you might want to remember the next time someone catches you talking to yourself. The fact is, every normal person enjoys good conversation. And in a pinch, if he runs out of people to talk to, he'll talk to himself.

But it's believed that few people ever learn the art of successful conversation. Those who do are very popular wherever they go. Being a good conversationalist is a little like walking a tightrope: it must be done in perfect balance. A good conversationalist is not only a good speaker with a wide range of interests and knowledge; he is also an excellent, interested listener and very comfortable to be around.

He refuses to be swept up into arguments and respects the opinions of others, even if they are at sharp variance with his own. He seems to know that conversation—good conversation—is not an exercise in debating a subject but, rather, in discussing it. He never jumps up and waves his arms or tries to shout down another person or make another person appear stupid or ridiculous.

The good conversationalist never loses his sense of humor or flexibility. He will bend gracefully when the discussion is going against his point of view. And he'll wait with attentive good humor until others have completed what they want to say. He will then come back with an opening comment, such as "I can certainly see the validity of your point of view." Then with the opposition disarmed for the moment, he will try to present his case in a gentle, more telling way.

And if he sees the conversation is headed for trouble, he will try to head it off into more agreeable areas. If he fails in this, he will simply stay out of it.

And invariably the best conversationalist is the best listener. Albert Einstein was once asked to define success, and he said, "If

A equals success, then the formula is A equals X plus Y plus Z. X is work. Y is play. Z is keep your mouth shut."

As T. S. Eliot wrote in his play *The Cocktail Party,* "Most of the trouble in the world is caused by people wanting to be important."

The good conversationalist does not want to be important. He wants the person or persons to whom he's talking to have a good time and to enjoy thinking about and discussing an interesting subject. He puts others and the subject matter ahead of himself. And his conversation is such that it camouflages him and highlights the subject and the others present.

As a result, he emerges from it all as a person to whom people are naturally attracted, perhaps without knowing why. He's always high on the invitation list.

Good conversation is an art and, like any art, must be learned. As in learning anything, listening is the best way to go about it. We not only make friends this way; we might even learn something.

YOUR GREATEST ASSET

Are you comfortable listening to others?

Do you always try to steer the conversation back to the other person?

Practice seeing how much you can learn through the fine art of listening.

I Might Be Wrong, But...

AUTHOR LEROY RAMSEY SAID, "Speaking with passion but without the facts is like making a beautiful dive into an empty pool." To convince or persuade others to come closer to your point of view, you have to base your opinion on incontestable facts that are honestly come by and readily grasped. As someone else put it, "make sure your mind is in gear before you set your mouth in motion."

Unless you can back up your argument with unassailable logic or know where you can get the facts, it is best to remain quiet or simply say, "In my opinion," and so on. Ben Franklin was a great one for that. He said that one of the greatest lessons he ever learned in winning others over to his side of a question was to begin everything he said with the words, "I may be wrong about this, but it seems to me..." and the combination of humbleness of attitude, linked with overwhelming logic, quickly had people assuring him that he was absolutely right.

To take the stand that you're right, even before you've made your point, is to make sure others will oppose you. It's also a sign of immaturity. "Speaking with passion but without the facts is like making a beautiful dive into an empty pool," and it has brought many otherwise intelligent people into positions of embarrassment, even disaster. In fact, it killed William Jennings Bryan, I believe.

We've all been guilty of it. "It seems to me..." are magic words. They soften and clear the way; they open others' minds and dispositions toward us. And then, if we're proven wrong, we're not so far out on the limb that we can't get back with good grace. But more important even than the escape route that it holds in readiness for us, it does not offend others and it helps bring them around to our way of thinking.

Avoiding an Argument

> *I have found that an argument, like a potential highway accident, can generally be spotted from some distance away, and it can be avoided the same way: slow down and approach with caution.*

HERE'S A WONDERFUL WAY to avoid an argument: simply ask questions. Instead of jumping in and disagreeing before you know any more about the subject under discussion and the other party, ask the person to state his case, specifically, and to define his terms. People who like to argue—and who will do so at the drop of a word on any subject—are people who enjoy ruffling the feelings of others. Willard Sloan once wrote an article, entitled "Arguments Don't Win Friends," in which he points out that arguments are useless and largely ridiculous. They're more a matter of temper than temperate conversation and discussion.

Subjects such as politics and religion can almost always provoke an argument. Racial prejudices can bring forth the most ridiculous statements in the form of arguments for or against certain practices. But if you'll apply this rule—to make your opponent be specific about some point you know backward and forward—you may avoid a foolish and endless fight, the kind of argument where nobody wins.

I have found that an argument, like a potential highway accident, can generally be spotted from some distance away, and it can be avoided the same way: slow down and approach with caution. In conversation, as in your car, the worst danger is speed. It's pretty hard to get seriously hurt going ten miles per hour. And you can avoid a serious argument that could lead to a lot of heartache just by being extremely careful when you come upon a situation that's likely to erupt into a serious argument.

If someone makes a statement that you feel is wrong or ridiculous, you should not remain silent. As you feel the adrenaline pumping into your system, instead of jumping on the other person with both feet, just ask, "Why do you say that?" If you get another absurd generalization, ask, "Would you mind being specific about that?" Ask questions such as "Why?" and "How do you know?" Instead of trying to prove your opponent wrong, make him prove himself right or discredit himself, which he will probably do if he's skating on thin ice. Put the burden of proof squarely where it belongs—on the shoulders of the person who started it.

Then you can sit back calmly and enjoy yourself while he gets in over his head, flounders in the swamp for a while, and finally tries to change the subject—no argument. And he won't be so quick to start another one the next time.

Robert McNamara, one of the nation's top executives, asks, "Why?" when something is proposed, even if he is immediately against the proposal. He wants all the facts. Perhaps he's been wrong about it, and if he's right, he forces the person making the proposal to prove its merits.

Now, no one can even guess at the number of families living between arguments in a state of unnecessary and uneasy truce. Since it takes two to argue, let's make sure we're not one of them. All we need to say is, "Why do you say that?" or "Exactly what do you mean by what you just said? What is your proof?" Keep the ball and the pressure on the person who is driving recklessly. It works like a charm, and you come out of it looking professional, wise, and levelheaded.

The Most Accessible of Pleasures

THE GREAT ROBERT LOUIS STEVENSON once wrote, "Talk is by far the most accessible of pleasures. It costs nothing in money, it is all profit, it completes our education, founds and fosters our friendships, and can be enjoyed at any age and in almost any state of health."

In Carl Sagan's marvelous book Broca's Brain, we learn that it was a French physician, Dr. Broca, who first discovered that portion of the human brain responsible for human speech. It came late in our development and is given complete responsibility for our having invented civilization.

Without articulate speech, we would simply be howling and grunting like the beasts in the jungle. Writing could not have been invented, nor information passed along from one generation to another. We would have nothing at all that we have today, other than our bodies, had it not been for the development of intelligible speech. It's an astounding, miraculous kind of thing.

And it's why our speech to one another plays such an important part in our lives. I once had a long talk with a young man, age sixteen, who was planning to become an architect. He was a very good student and quite serious about his education. He told me he found math easy, but he was having a hard time with English. It's been my experience that that is often the case and works much the same in the reverse. Students with a facility for English often find math difficult.

I explained to him why giving his English studies a lot of attention was so important. I told him that as an architect, he would still be dealing orally with the people necessary for his success. Additionally, he would be expected to write letters, prepare written presentations, and so on. He would find that his ability to use his language would be called upon far more than his skills as an architect. None of us can work in a vacuum, nor want to. We interface with hundreds of other people. And it is our mastery of our language that determines their consideration and evaluation of us.

It is not done consciously. I doubt if few people even think about it once during their lives. But it is a fact nonetheless that our use of our language determines, to an enormous extent, our place in human society. As an architect, I told him, he would be dealing with other university people on a daily basis. His business clients would evaluate him on the basis of their contact with him.

He didn't have to become an expert in the use of English; that was for English teachers. But he must have a large and flexible vocabulary and an unconscious ease with his language. He must not have to think about it too much as he spoke. His ideas and responses must flow from him with facility. That's all. And I believe we parted with his having a new respect for that hated subject in school. I wish more English teachers would give students the whole story on why our speech is so vitally important to our lives.

Chapter Four

Improving Your Writing Skills

On Persuading the Multitude

In the *Dialogues*, Plato says, "Gorgias, what is there greater than the word that persuades the judges in the courts, or the senators in the council, or the citizens in the assembly, or at any other political meeting? If you have the power of uttering this word, you will have the physician your slave, and the trainer your slave, and the money-maker of whom you talk will be found to gather treasures, not for himself, but for you who are able to speak and to persuade the multitude."

As so much that we read in Plato, it's as true today as it was then: the person who has an excellent command of the language has tremendous advantage over those who do not—especially in getting jobs and moving quickly up the ranks. In politics, it is of particular advantage in getting elected, surely; and getting what you want done after you get there; and in getting re-elected.

I've seen it happen hundreds of times in meetings—business meetings, executive meetings, all kinds of meetings: the person who can stand on his feet and make an excellent and articulate presentation wins the admiration of everyone, and he is marked for advancement by his superiors. On the other hand, a person who misuses or fumbles and mumbles the language—even though that person is bright and competent—is at a distinct disadvantage. He's at a disadvantage because a prime prerequisite of management is the ability to communicate clearly and effectively and to motivate those in one's charge.

In difficult situations, the person with a first-class command of his language can usually extricate himself without too much damage and difficulty. Now perhaps it should not be this way, but there is no doubt that it is, whether we like it or not.

Looks, too, make a tremendous difference. They shouldn't, but they clearly do. It's been found that good-looking people have a much better chance in court—especially with juries—and it applies to men as well as women. Juries tend to think good-looking people are less apt to be guilty—or if they are guilty, less apt to be at fault or to go on committing other crimes. It's a fact that everyone looks with more favor on good-looking people. They tend to advance more quickly in business, all other things being equal.

We can't do a great deal about our looks, that being our ancestral plight—for good or bad or somewhere in between. But we can certainly, any of us, obtain an excellent command of the language. That's simply a matter of study. It can be learned in the same way one learns any other subject—by reading books on the subject, by assiduously looking up words one does not understand, and by reading aloud until one develops a well-modulated, clearly enunciated way of speaking.

More than anything else, it depends simply on understanding how important our speech is and giving it the attention it deserves. We don't have to become professors of English to have excellent speaking habits, to speak clearly and use actual words for what we mean instead of dumb comments such as "you know" or "you know what I mean." The facts seem to be that people don't know what you mean unless you state it clearly and effectively.

How to Sell Your Ideas

ELMER WHEELER, the famous "Sell the sizzle, not the steak" man, had some good advice about how to sell your ideas.

Have you ever approached your boss with a red-hot idea for increasing efficiency, only to have him become resentful instead of enthusiastic? Have you ever offered your wife or husband or the neighbors so-called good advice? If you have, you know what I mean when I say that people resent having other people's ideas forced on them.

When someone approaches us with a new idea, our instinctive reaction is to put up a defense against it. We feel that we must protect our individuality and the status quo, and most of us are egotistical enough to think that our ideas are better than someone else's.

There are three tested rules for putting your ideas across to other people so as to arouse their enthusiasm. Here they are:

Rule 1: Use a fly rod, not a feeding tube. Others won't accept your idea until they can accept it as their idea. When you want to sell someone an idea, take a lesson from the fisherman who casts his fly temptingly near the trout. He could never ram the hook into the trout's mouth. But he can entice the trout to come to the hook.

Don't appear too anxious to have your ideas accepted. Just bring them out where they can be seen. You might say, "Have you considered this?" instead of "This is the way." "Do you think this idea would work?" is better than "Here's what we should do." Let the other person sell himself on your idea. Then he'll stay sold.

Rule 2: Let the other person argue your case for you. He instinctively feels called upon to raise some objection to save face. Give him a chance to disagree with you—by presenting your own objections.

"The way to convince another," said Ben Franklin, "is to state your case moderately and accurately. Then say that, of course, you may be mistaken about it, which causes your listener to receive what you have to say and, like as not, turn about and convince you of it, since you are in doubt. But if you go at him in a tone of positiveness and arrogance, you only make an opponent of him."

Abraham Lincoln used the same technique in selling his idea to a jury. He argued both sides of the case, but there was always the subtle suggestion that his side was the logical one. An opposing lawyer said of him, "He made a better statement of my case to the jury than I could have made myself."

Rule 3: Ask; don't tell. Patrick Henry, another famous idea salesman, knew how to do this. In his famous "Liberty or Death" Speech, he asked, "Our brethren are already in the field! Why stand we here idle? ...What would they have? Is life so dear or peace so sweet as to be purchased at the price of chains and slavery?" Try saying the same thing in positive statements, and see how much antagonism it would invoke.

One: Do not force the other person to accept your idea; rather, entice him to come to it himself. Two: Let the other person argue your case for you by not being too sure. And three: Ask; don't tell. It's very good advice, I think. Don't you?

Are They Buying What You're Offering?

Our main purpose is to get the people to buy what we have to say. We're not trying to win prizes as orators, arm swingers, or podium thumpers. We're there to sell the people on an idea, to transfer our enthusiasm for our subject to our listeners.

WE ALL REMEMBER funny and far out advertising campaigns that had the whole country laughing, but tests after the campaigns showed no appreciable gain in sales. The test of all communication is "Does it sell the product?" Now, this kind of rule can, of course, be abused. Tedious, ridiculous and hateful ad campaigns have been excused by the advertising people who say, "Well, it sells the product." Selling the product is the idea, but not at all costs—not at the cost of good taste, good manners, or good morals. But still we must sell the product, and that's where burning the midnight oil comes into play.

That's where study, experience, trial and error, deep knowledge, and education all count in our favor. We want to sell our ideas, but we don't want to get so cute or clever in doing so that the people concentrate on the smoke screen and fail to get the point of it all, fail to see and/or buy what we're trying to sell—the reason for all the sound and fury.

Originality and creativity are of tremendous importance here. Now, that applies to the preacher and his sermon, the father or mother talking to the kids, selling them on the good life, better way to live, pitfalls to avoid. It applies to selling ourselves to our superiors and our fellow workers and subordinates, and it applies to the actual selling of our organization's product or service. Now, when we accept an invitation to make a speech, we accept the challenge to sell our ideas to others.

Our main purpose is to get the people to buy what we have to say. We're not trying to win prizes as orators, arm swingers, or podium thumpers. We're there to sell the people on an idea, to transfer our enthusiasm for our subject to our listeners.

That's why I think it's a good idea to go easy on the jokes. In all speeches, except those of a very serious nature, there are perfectly natural places for a funny line or two. Adding that line and getting the audience to laugh and relax is good, but it should remain subsidiary to your theme and purpose. If there is the slightest doubt in your mind as to whether or not to use a funny line or a joke, by all means leave it out. When it's right, you'll know it. It will fit like a glove. It will be perfect.

After giving a speech, it would be great if we could poll the members of the audience and ask them a few questions like "In one sentence, what was the theme of my talk?" and then the big questions, such as "Did you buy what I talked about here today?"

I had a man come up to me at a social gathering not long ago. He introduced himself and said, "I've heard you speak, Mr. Nightingale, and you make a very interesting talk. I don't buy what you're selling, but it's a very interesting talk." I immediately put him down as a crackpot or a total moron, but I smiled and shook his hand

and said something such as, "Well, you can't sell everybody." But I felt a stab of failure all the same, and I knew he wasn't a moron—a crackpot, maybe.

It's hard for us to imagine that any rational person on the face of the globe could find disagreement with our devastating logic, supported as it is with indisputable facts and buttressed with overwhelming reason. But they do. Some of them do. I wanted to say to my criticizer, "You could have easily come up with a friendlier comment than that." But he was right. He obviously had not bought what I had to say that morning. The applause after my talk had convinced me that I'd make a sale. Obviously, I had not sold everyone, and it helps us to realize it.

And you won't either. People who drive a certain make of car can't understand why everyone doesn't drive that make. Republicans are amazed that rational, intelligent human beings can belong to the Democratic Party, and vice versa.

People drive dozens of makes of cars, believe in many different ways, are devoutly loyal to hundreds of various religions and sects. And you and I can jump up and down on the stage until we drop over from exhaustion trying to change their beliefs—and very probably to no avail. But when we have something to say, we can do our very best to persuade them to buy what we're trying to sell. If we persuade some of them, we're doing fine. If we persuade most of them, we're true spellbinders and can top the best salespeople. But we're not going to sell all of them, I don't think, all of the time.

But it's good to remember that that's the name of the communication game—to sell an idea, to get the good people to actually buy what we're selling.

On Writing

IF YOU'VE EVER HAD the urge to write but felt you couldn't because you didn't know enough about the English language, forget it and start writing. The trick—and it isn't easy—is to write the same way you talk. The reason I say it isn't easy is because it's difficult to learn to read and sound as though you're not reading but talking in a normal, conversational manner.

Have you ever heard an inexperienced person being interviewed for a so-called "spontaneous" commercial? Sure you have, and you know darn well he's reading from a cue card, a script, or has memorized his speech.

It's the same with writing letters, or for those of us who are neurotic enough to want to write for a living. Don't worry about splitting infinitives, dangling participles, or using prepositions to end a sentence with. All that stuff has long gone out the window. Today, conversational English is the secret to, if not good, at least enjoyable and possibly salable writing. Personally, I think enjoyable, interesting writing is good writing.

For a long time now, people have been putting forth an effort to take the formality and stiffness out of their business letters, and it's really not difficult if they'll just dictate their letters the same way they normally talk. If they received a letter from a customer and called him on the phone, they would never think of saying, "Thank you for your letter on the fifteenth. After due consideration, we have reached the conclusion…" and so on. Instead, they'd say something like, "I got your letter, and after thinking it over, I've decided to go ahead."

The next time you write a letter, try putting down the words just as you'd say them if the person to whom you're writing is sitting across the table. Use lots of contractions and apostrophes, just as you would in conversation. Don't write "cannot" if you would naturally say "can't"; don't write "do not" when you'd normally say "don't," nor "let us" when you'd say "let's."

And if you've got a story you want to write, sit down and write it as though you were telling it to an old friend or a youngster. Write as long as the writing comes easily and naturally. Stop when it becomes forced and unnatural. Gradually, you can increase the periods of productive writing and probably stretch them in time to three or four hours. Did you know that four double-spaced typewritten pages a day will turn out the equivalent of a full-sized novel in three months?

You might remember what Leo Tolstoy said: "A writer is dear and necessary for us only in the measure in which he reveals to us the inner working of his soul."

Simplicity Is the Key

I USED TO KNOW A MAN, who was one of the principals of a large and very successful advertising agency, who had a hard-and-fast rule against clichés. A cliché, as you know, is a trite phrase that has lost its meaning through constant use but that often becomes so much of a habit with us that we use it automatically, without thinking about it. I used one, just for fun, in my opening sentence. Did you notice it? I said "who had a hard-and-fast rule against clichés." What is a "hard-and-fast rule"? It's much better to say, "He had a rule against clichés." The words "hard and fast" are unnecessary. In advertising, they take up valuable space and increase the cost without adding a thing to the message.

Some time back, we went through a two-page letter, just for fun, and by cutting only the superfluous words, reduced it to a one-page letter consisting of just three paragraphs. Not only was about 70 percent of the letter completely unnecessary, but the new edition was fast, lean, and muscular. The original letter was fat, unwieldy, and full of clichés—phrases that you put into letters without even realizing you're doing it. We have a tendency to speak the same way. Have you ever noticed how often you hear people say, "I mean"? If you simply say what you mean, you don't have to tell anyone what you're doing. Other examples are "stuff like that," or "you know what I mean," or "in other words," or "like I said." And one time I had a cab driver in Philadelphia who, after every sentence, would look around and ask, "Am I right or wrong?"

There's nothing particularly wrong about this, but it does add a lot of unnecessary weight and excess baggage to something that can be simple, direct, clean, and powerful.

It's been said that the late Ernest Hemingway would sometimes spend most of a complete morning writing a single paragraph. And if you read Hemingway, you'll notice his effectiveness in saying what he wants to say in the fewest possible words.

Another example is the Sermon on the Mount found in the Bible—more than 70 percent of Jesus's great address consists of one-syllable words.

The next time you write a letter—particularly a business letter—see if you can do a better job by using simple, strong, hardworking words. Cut out all clichés such as "however," or "with reference to your letter," and all those silly windups. Whenever you write a letter, read it over and ask yourself if you talk like that. If not, don't write like that. And join the crusade against clichés, bromides, and old sayings that have no meaning or value. Some of them, like fine old bridges, we want to keep, especially ones such as "Heaven helps those who help themselves."

How to Get Started Writing

SUCCESS AS A WRITER is the same as in any other field—it's a matter of forming the right habits. And the best way to form the right habits is to do something you know you should be doing, every day.

You know, the person who writes a daily column for the newspaper, the cartoonist with a daily syndicated feature, or perhaps the Hollywood script writer on a definite assignment sooner or later finds himself drawing a blank. That is, with a deadline approaching—a deadline that must be met—he finds himself without a single idea. The same thing happens to me. It happens very rarely, but it happens. You put a piece of paper in the typewriter and then stare at it. You let your mind wander...you concentrate...you glance around your library...you read something. Then you begin to think of all the things you'd rather be doing...fishing maybe, or playing golf, or traveling to some distant place. You forcibly bring your mind back to the job at hand and start the whole thing all over again.

There's the typewriter with the blank sheet in it, and there's the approaching deadline. Do you know what you do? You begin to write. You just begin!

This is why the professional writer laughs when he hears someone say, "I have to wait for the mood. I must court the muse and wait for inspiration." The men and women who earn their living writing against deadlines would starve, or find some other business, if they wanted for inspiration.

One time, some years ago, I spoke before a university journalism class. One of the comments I made was later to come back and haunt me. I told them that if they were really serious about writing—writing for a living—they should write something every day. Even if it was nothing more than making a few notes on the back of an envelope—write something every day. And if they found they couldn't think of anything to write, to write anyway.

I still believe I was right, but there have been many times when I've sat and stared at a blank sheet of paper for four or five hours before I could write a single word. Success as a writer is the same as in any other field—it's a matter of forming the right habits. And the best way to form the right habits is to do something you know you should be doing, every day. The more you do it, the easier it becomes, the more competent and confident you become, and the work becomes steadily better. Also, the more you do it, the more ideas you get for future work.

I guess we all know that the longer you put off what you know very well you should be doing, the more you dread doing it. Finally, because of our procrastination, the job looms far larger than it did in the beginning until we finally, in a kind of desperation, pitch into it and discover that it really wasn't nearly as bad as we thought it was going to be. We should have done it at once, in the beginning, without wasting all that time—storing up all that apprehension and being miserable from sidestepping our responsibilities.

I'm willing to make a guess right now that you've got something you should have done days or maybe even weeks ago, but you've been putting it off, hoping it would go away. If you don't mind taking some advice from a person who makes it a practice to do the same thing—do it now! Just pitch in and start. Before you know it, it'll be finished, and you'll feel really proud of yourself—until the next time.

You know, if every day each of us would just do the things we know very well we really should be doing we'd always be ahead of the game, instead of lagging forever behind and then having to run like mad to catch up.

Chapter Five

Learning to Cultivate Your Creativity

Using Imagination to Fuel Your Life

IMAGINATION IS EVERYTHING. I can't remember who wrote those three words in that order, but it seems to sum it up. Imagination is everything. Our lives will reflect the way we use our imagination. The child imagines himself walking like the adults he sees above him. As soon as he can walk, he wants to run. As we reach successive plateaus in life, we begin to imagine ourselves reaching the next one. And that's our imagination. It leads us on from one idea to another through every day and every year of our lives.

But if we're not careful, our imaginations can lead us into mazes of confused complications from which we may find it difficult to extricate ourselves. So it's a good idea, as we use our imagination, to always strive for simplicity, to avoid the complicated.

Are we living the lives we want to live? Or are we living stereotyped lives based on phony values?

Usually, they're a combination of both—a kind of compromise that says, "Surely other people must have some idea of what constitutes 'the good life.' After all, there are so many of them." But when we look closer, we see that they're living "shadow lives," as Lewis Mumford calls them. In competitive ice skating, you've seen a couple match each other's movements almost perfectly. It's called "shadow skating," I believe, meaning each might be the other's shadow. In any sort of neighborhood, you will tend to find people living much the same way. Their homes, landscaping, furnishings, and lives are typified, if by anything at all, by an almost total lack of imagination. Imagination, like anything else, needs fuel for production. You can't have something from nothing. Thomas Edison said, "I'm a sponge. I want to know the answer to everything." With his great lifetime inventory of information, he could assemble an incredible array of new combinations and permutations.

Electric light is a combination of elements, and so is any good idea—or any bad idea for that matter. Most of us make the mistake of not asking *why*. Why do I live here in this house rather than in some other house? Why this life instead of another life? Why this work instead of other work? Why these rewards instead of others? Now this doesn't mean we'll change anything necessarily, but at least we'll be living lives that have been examined and found to be to our personal liking. We'll know that we're not living the lives we're living simply because they reflect and are pretty much composite copies of the lives we see about us.

These questions should be, to my way of thinking, deep main currents in our lives—our family lives, our work and our leisure, and our rewards in the form of income. Our family lives should be good and richly satisfying. What is our input here? How are we using our imagination to bring meaning, charm, and love to our family relationships? It's an ongoing process that should become richer and more meaningful with the passing of time.

How about your home? Is it what you want? H. L. Mencken once commented that the average home is a house of horrors and doesn't reflect poor taste so much as it reflects no taste at all. People tend to order their steaks medium and their homes and lives the same way. Medium rhymes with tedium.

The family is the most important part of the lives of most of us. What good is accomplishment if there's no one with whom to share it? What good is anything if there's no one with whom to share it? And since the family is first in importance, it represents a fertile field for the imagination—not just for the woman in the family, but for the man and hopefully for the kids as well. Family creative thinking sessions are a lot of fun and a never-ending source of good ideas. Check every idea for basic simplicity. Avoid complication whenever possible.

No matter what it is we want, if it's within the realm of reality we can get it through imagination applied to our work. Nothing now being done by man is being done the way it can and will be. Everything will be done much better—not *can* be; *will* be—whether it's the result of our applied imagination or not. People who resist change in their work are impediments to progress, yet the first words the new person on the job usually hears are, "Now this is the way it's done around here."

A business leader made the comment that "if we're doing anything this year the way it was done last year, we're obsolete." Now that's an extreme generalization, but it deserves careful attention; and in most cases, it's true.

Following the Follower

Habit patterns and ways of thinking become deeply established, and it seems easier and more comforting to follow them than to cope with change, even when change may represent freedom and achievement.

PROCESSIONARY CATERPILLARS TRAVEL in long undulating lines, one creature behind the other. Jean-Henri Fabre, the French entomologist, once led a group of these caterpillars onto the rim of a large flowerpot so that the leader of the procession found himself nose to tail with the last caterpillar in the procession, forming a circle without end or beginning.

Through sheer force of habit and, of course, instinct, the ring of caterpillars circled the flowerpot for seven days and seven nights until they died from exhaustion and starvation. An ample supply of food was close at hand and plainly visible, but it was outside the range of the circle, so the caterpillars continued along the beaten path.

People often behave in a similar way. Habit patterns and ways of thinking become deeply established, and it seems easier and more comforting to follow them than to cope with change, even when change may represent freedom and achievement.

If someone shouts, "Fire!" it is automatic to blindly follow the crowd, and many thousands have needlessly died because of it. How many stop and ask themselves, "Is this really the best way out of here?"

So many people miss the boat because it's easier and more comforting to follow—to follow without questioning the qualifications of the people just ahead—than to do some independent thinking and checking.

A hard thing for most people to fully understand is that people in such numbers can be so wrong, like the caterpillars going around and around the edge of the flowerpot, with life and food just a short distance away. "If most people are living that way, it must be right," they think. But a little checking will reveal that throughout all recorded history, the majority of mankind has an unbroken record of being wrong about most things, especially the important things.

It's difficult for people to come to the understanding that only a small minority of people ever really get the word about life, about living abundantly and successfully. Success in the important departments of life seldom comes naturally—no more naturally than success at anything: a musical instrument, sports, fly-fishing, tennis, golf, business, marriage, parenthood, landscape gardening. But somehow people wait passively for success to come to them, like the caterpillars going around in circles, waiting for sustenance, following nose to tail, living as other people are living in their unspoken, tacit assumption that other people know how to live successfully.

It's a good idea to step out of the line every once in a while and look up ahead to see if the line is going where we want it to go. If it is, it could be the first time.

A Profile of the Creative Person

WE'VE FOUND THAT creative people, though they may be dissimilar in many respects, have certain attitudes and employ certain techniques to their own benefit and to the benefit of us all.

I'd like now to use these techniques and attitudes as the basis for a descriptive sketch of a creative person.

As we go through this sketch, I'd like you to think about this person. Where and when have you seen him or her? Is this a person you know at work, or in your neighborhood, or right at home?

It will be helpful to read this message frequently and be reminded of these techniques and attitudes, which, if practiced regularly, will result in your living an even more creative, rewarding life. Another good idea is to project the image of the creative person onto your

Learning to Cultivate Your Creativity

own actions; then judge for yourself what areas could stand some improvement.

First of all, the creative person realizes that his mind is an inexhaustible storehouse. It can provide anything he earnestly wants in life. But in order to draw from this storehouse, he must constantly augment its stock of information, thoughts, and wisdom. His mind gives him ideas, and ideas solve problems.

The person we're talking about has a carefully thought-out and clearly defined set of goals toward which he's working. By knowing where he's going—and determining to get there—he gives meaning and purpose to his daily work, to everything he does. He never wastes time "just drifting." He's always in control of his life.

The creative person knows his brain thrives on exercise, so he uses a part of each day for thinking imaginatively about three things: himself, his words, and his fellow man. By asking himself questions involving these three areas, he's prospecting in the richest gold mine ever known. And the answers to his questions are often ideas that he can put into immediate action.

He reaches out for ideas. He respects the minds of others, gives credit to their mental abilities. Everyone has ideas; they're free, and many of them are excellent. By first listening to the ideas and then thinking them through before judging them, the creative person avoids prejudice and closed-mindedness. This is the way he maintains a creative "climate" around himself.

You know, ideas are like slippery fish. They seem to have a peculiar knack of getting away from us. Because of this, the creative person always has a pad and pencil handy. When he gets an idea, he writes it down. He knows that many people have found their whole lives changed by a single great thought. By capturing ideas immediately, he doesn't risk forgetting them.

And these "captured" ideas are deposited in "idea banks," eight-and-a-half- by eleven-inch envelopes that are labeled with topics of interest. A friend of mine, a very successful writer, writes his books this way. He labels each envelope with the name of a chapter. Then, whenever he gets an idea or finds new material, he sees that it gets into the proper envelope. Before long, his book has practically written itself.

Having a sincere interest in people, our creative person listens carefully when someone else is talking. He's intensely observant, absorbing everything he sees and hears. He behaves as if everyone he meets wears a sign that reads, "I am the more important person on earth." Thus, he makes it a point always to talk with other people's interests in mind. And it pays off in a flood of new ideas and information that would otherwise be lost to him forever.

Widening his circle of friends and broadening his base of knowledge are two more very effective techniques of the creative person.

If he's staying at a hotel where there's a convention not allied to his own work, he'll drop in on it, make new friends, and listen for ideas that might help him. He's always looking for better ways to do his work and live his life.

The creative person anticipates achievement. He expects to win. And the above-average production engendered by this kind of attitude affects those around him in a positive way. He's a plus factor for all who know him.

You know, problems are challenges to creative minds. Without problems, there would be little reason to think at all. Welcoming them as normal and predictable parts of living singles him out as an above-average person. He knows it's a waste of time merely to worry about problems, so he wisely invests the same time and energy into solving problems.

He can even avoid problems by anticipating potentially troublesome areas and doing something about them before they turn sour on him.

The research and development departments of many leading companies are constantly involved in exactly this sort of advance planning.

The creative person knows the value of giving himself and his ideas away. He's a "go-giver" as well as a "go-getter." The hand that gives always gathers, and doing things for other people is a vital part of his way of life.

When the creative person gets an idea, he puts it through a series of steps designed to improve it. He thinks in new directions. He builds big ideas from little ones, new ideas from old ones, associating ideas, combing them, adapting, substituting, magnifying, minifying, rearranging, and reversing ideas.

He steers clear of mind-weakeners: noise, fatigue, needless worry, unbalanced diets, over-indulgence in food or drink, and people with negative attitudes.

He asks polite, probing questions that bolster the ego and expand the mind. Questions are the creative acts of the intelligence, and he uses them often and to everyone's advantage.

And the creative person uses his spare time wisely. He knows that many great ideas, books, and inventions were conceived during the creator's spare time. We all have the same number of minutes in a day, and the creative person values each one of them.

YOUR GREATEST ASSET

A creative person has:

a clearly defined set of goals toward which he or she is working,

a pad and pencil handy for ideas that are deposited into "idea banks,"

good listening skills when someone else is talking,

a widening circle of friends and a broad knowledge base,

an expectation of winning,

an understanding of the value of giving oneself and one's ideas away,

an ability to put ideas through a series of steps to improve them,

and an ability to make wise use of his or her time.

Learning to Cultivate Your Creativity

What Drives the Creative Person

CREATIVE AND PRODUCTIVE PEOPLE are not creative and productive for the benefit of others. It's because they're driven by the need to be creative and productive. They'd be creative and productive if they each lived on a deserted island and simply had to stack what each produced in a big pile with no one benefiting from or even aware of what he was doing. You'll hear people say that we're happiest when we're serving others, and that's true—but it's not true because of any great altruism on our part. It's true because we experience the joy of producing something. That others benefit from it is fine, but only secondary.

It's good to know that others benefit from and enjoy what we produce. There's satisfaction in that—ego satisfaction and the desire to produce more. If everyone continually rejected our creative or productive efforts, we might become sullen and resentful. We might even stop all efforts for a while. But eventually we'd begin to produce again in a hope that at some point someone would see the sense of what we're doing.

That is the story of the painters who were before their time. Renoir was laughed at and rejected not only by the public but by his own fellow artists. We look at a painting by Renoir today and marvel that anything so fine and beautiful could ever be an object of scorn. And he painted thousands of paintings. He went on producing them. When he brought one of his canvases to one of the most eminent Parisian teachers, the expert glanced at the work and said, "You are, I presume, dabbling in paint to arouse yourself." And Renoir replied, "Of course. When it ceases to amuse me, I'll stop painting." Everything he painted delighted him, and he painted everything.

Even Manet said to Monet, "Renoir has no talent at all. You who are his friend should tell him kindly to give up painting." A group of artists who were rejected by the establishment of their time formed their own association in self-defense. Do you know who was in that group? They were Degas, Pissarro, Monet, Cézanne, and Renoir—five of the greatest artists of all time, all doing what they believed in, in the face of total rejection.

Since we're on the subject of Renoir, in his later life he suffered terribly from rheumatism, especially in his hands. He lived in constant pain. And when Matisse visited the aging painter, he saw that every stroke was causing renewed pain, and he asked, "Why do you still have to work? Why continue to torture yourself?" And then Renoir answered, "The pain passes, but the pleasure, the creation of beauty, remains." One day when he was seventy-eight and quite famous and successful finally, he said, "I'm still making progress." And the next day he was dead.

This is the mark of the creative, productive person—still making progress, still learning, still producing as long as he lives, despite pain or problems of all kinds; not producing for the joy or satisfaction of others, but because he must—because it gave him pleasure and satisfaction.

The Most Valuable Tools of Creative People

INSIDE THE MIND of each person we meet there is some knowledge that could benefit us if only we could learn what it is. Open-ended questions let people know we want to hear their ideas, opinions, and thoughts.

Creative people are invariably intelligent people. And they're curious—about themselves, those around them, and the world in which they live. This is the kind of curiosity that has been called one of the permanent and certain characteristics of a vigorous intellect.

Questions are the creative acts of the intelligence, and the questions that work the hardest for us and bring us the greatest amount of useful information are the open-ended questions. Now, these are questions that can't be answered with a simple "yes" or "no." They're asked by using the six W's, H, and I technique: who, what, when, where, why, which, how, and if.

Rudyard Kipling put it this way:

I keep six honest serving-men

(They taught me all I knew);

Their names are What and Why and When

And How and Where and Who.

All we're doing is adding two more: Which and If.

Now, this isn't entirely new to you. You employed the six W's, H, and I all the time when you were a child. Have you ever tried to count the number of times each day a four- or five-year-old uses the word "why"? You see, each question a child asks is an attempt to add to his limited knowledge. When adults lose patience with this constant barrage of questions, a child either finds some other way of getting the information or just forgets the whole thing, thereby neglecting a valuable tool he'll want later in life—the open-ended question.

Now, as adults we know that inside the mind of each person we meet there is some knowledge that could benefit us if only we could learn what it is. The open-ended question technique really opens people up. By asking open-ended questions, we get people to remove the barriers that normally keep the information out of our grasp.

Human beings like to talk about things that interest them. Open-ended questions let people know we want to hear their ideas, opinions, and thoughts. Each of us has two ears and one mouth. And it seems to be a good idea to do at least twice as much listening as talking. An old Texas friend of mine used to say, "You ain't learnin' nothin' while you're talkin.'"

But the object of asking open-ended questions isn't merely to get other people to talk. We could spend days standing around gabbing with people who have very little to say that would benefit us. Instead, the object of our who-what-when-where-why-which-how-if questions is to gather, absorb, and utilize that information that will be useful to us—move us ahead in fields of our own interests and endeavors. But in so doing, we're also employing the best technique known for making friends, for success in human relations, and for selling our own ideas. Oddly enough, the more we listen, the better conversationalist we seem to the person doing the talking.

One of this country's top newsmen set a good example of this kind of purposeful questioning. He knew how to ask open-ended questions so provocatively that he could almost always get world leaders to give him exclusive interviews. His wise questions earned him the highest position in his field—that of chief executive for one of the great news services.

And the open-ended question is equally useful to the businessman. Suppose, for instance, that you've just met a Mr. Smith, who is an official of a company operating in an area different from your own. Instead of talking about the weather, you might ask him, "Mr. Smith, how did you get into your line of work?" Now, here's a man who obviously has some degree of success in business, so you stand an excellent chance of learning something that will be useful to you.

One of the best salesmen I know uses open-ended questions to great advantage when he's talking with a prospect. Instead of saying, "We make the best thingumabob in the world," he asks, "Mr. Prospect, when you buy thingumabobs, what features are most important to you?" Here's an effective method for taking people off the offensive—for getting them to talk to your advantage. This technique works well for anyone who'll give some thought to what he's going to say rather than just blurting out the first thing that pops into his mind.

So, ask skillful, probing, open-ended questions. And ask them in a sincere, courteous manner. Anyone who uses the six W's, H, and I technique wisely, courteously, and with those people who can contribute something to his understanding will quickly find this to be one of his most useful creative techniques.

The best way I know to practice asking open-ended questions is to try out a few on myself. If this sounds like a good idea, you might want to try it, too. Ask yourself:

- Who has greater knowledge of my job than I?
- What can I do to learn some of the things he knows but I don't?
- Why must my job be done this way?
- And if there is a better way to do my job, what would it be?

Take time to ponder these questions. Their answers—the facts and information you will gain—can make your life infinitely more interesting and rewarding.

Whenever you talk with others, use lots of open-ended questions. They're your most valuable creative tools.

Thinking Techniques to Increase Creativity

WHAT ARE SOME OF the best techniques for using our creative faculties more effectively to solve problems, make decisions, achieve goals, and better fulfill our ultimate human responsibility, which is to think? Here are a few I have learned:

First, think association. An example of thinking association would be to associate names with familiar objects or words in order to remember them better. Two more examples of thinking association are the keyword and the association list techniques. The keyword technique is used by people who want to remember a series of ideas. They join the initial letters of the idea words together to form a simple keyword. By remembering the keyword, they can recall the whole series of ideas. An association list is used by memory experts to recall prodigious lists of articles by associating each one with another article in a previously memorized list. The creative person is forever associating ideas and continually searching for associative relationships.

Next, think combination. Almost everything in nature is a combination of elements. You're quite a combination yourself. Scientists calculate that if the energy in the hydrogen atoms of your body could be utilized, you could supply all the electrical needs of the entire country for nearly a week. A DuPont scientist says that the atoms of your body contain a potential energy of more than eleven million kilowatt hours per pound.

A simple pencil is a combination of wood, carbon, rubber, paint, and metal. A few more examples might include ham and eggs, pie à la mode, the radio-TV and film combination, and orbiting satellites combined with microwave telephone relay stations. Somebody dreamed up the idea of combining comedy and music, and musical comedy was born.

You can come up with some really great ideas by finding new combinations yourself. Everything you see, hear, touch, taste, and smell during the day offers an opportunity to consider new combinations. When you brush your teeth, you might think of a toothbrush that contains the toothpaste in the handle. You might combine your mirror with a motto reminding you to start the day right. It might read, "How can I increase my service today?" or "Today is the only time I've got. I'll use it well." So, let's think combination.

Next, think adaptation. Burlap fabric, originally used for making gunny sacks, has been adapted for drapes, wall coverings, and stylish dresses. (Some salesmen were thinking adaptation.) Airplane seat belts have been adapted for use in automobiles to bring new safety in highway driving. The tape recorder and motion picture, originally developed for entertainment, are today adapted for instruction and education. Rocket motors, which were developed to propel some missiles, have been adapted to lift peaceful space vehicles into orbital and interplanetary flight. During the next year, you are going to see the result of people thinking adaptation and coming up with ideas worth thousands of dollars. Why couldn't one of these people be you? The only limit to what you can achieve by adapting old products to new uses—old methods to new applications—is the limit of your own creativity.

Next, think substitution. When you think substitution, you ask yourself how you might substitute a different material or thing for the one now used. For example, plastic is used as a substitute for wood and metal. Aluminum is a substitute for other metals. Stainless steel is often substituted for chrome. The transistor often replaces the vacuum tube. Old, weathered planking can be used as a substitute for a conventional wall in a family room or study with dramatic and interesting effect. In short, don't assume that because a particular thing has always been used in the past that you have to use it now. Perhaps there's a substitute that will work better, or last longer, or cost less, or be lighter or more colorful, and so forth. Let's think substitution.

Next, think magnification. Think big! Examples: skyscrapers, the Pentagon, king-sized soft drinks, giant economy-size packages. What do you work with that might be made larger?

Or, think minification. Think small! Examples: the solar battery, the transistor, the compact car, tiny radios that fit into your pocket, small portable TV sets, smaller-sized food products. How about the bikini? That's certainly thinking small!

And now, to keep your mind moving—think rearrangement. That is, turn things around, backward, upside down, or inside out. An interesting example of this was when someone came up with the idea of putting the mink on the inside of a woman's coat—all the warmth, luxury, and status of full-length mink in a casual coat! And it's nothing more than a mink coat turned inside out.

Another good example of this is the building with its skeletal framework outside; the building is suspended inside. Insects have their skeletons outside; we have ours inside. They both work fine. What do you work with that can benefit from this kind of thinking? What can you turn around, revolutionize?

Rearrange things, change pace, alter sequence, think of modifying—changing color, motion, timing, sound, odor, taste, form, and shape. This type of thinking works for everyone. Salesmen use these creative techniques to discover new applications for products or services, new ways to emphasizing customer benefits, new ideas to solve customer problems, better ways to organize their time and effort.

Summing up: If you want to spur your mind to new action, think combination, association, adaptation, substitution, magnification, minification, and rearrangement.

If at first you force—literally force—your mind to think in all these seven ways, you'd probably be amazed with the ideas you develop. And before long, you'll find yourself thinking in each of these ways as a matter of course. This kind of thinking increases the scope of your mindpower and enables you to achieve fuller use of your brain. Your mind has an infinite variety of things it can do and an infinite capacity for work. Let it work for you. Take nothing for granted. Everything can and will be changed, improved. The only thing you can count on for certain is change. Don't wait for it. Be in the forefront; help bring it about.

Chapter Six

How to Apply Creativity to Problem-Solving

Creative Problem-Solving Using Lateral Thinking

HERE'S A LITTLE STORY to test how good of a thinker you are.

Many years ago, a merchant in London had the misfortune to owe a huge sum to a mean moneylender. The moneylender, who was old and ugly, fancied the merchant's beautiful, young daughter. He proposed a bargain. He said he would cancel the merchant's debt if he could have the girl instead.

Both the merchant and his daughter were horrified at the suggestion. So the cunning moneylender proposed that they let Providence decide the matter. He told them that he would put a black pebble and a while pebble into an empty money bag, and then the girl would have to pick out one of the pebbles. If she chose the black pebble, she would become his wife, and her father's debt would be canceled. If she chose the white pebble, she would stay with her father, and the debt would still be canceled. But if she refused to pick a pebble, her father would be thrown into jail, and she would starve.

Reluctantly, the merchant agreed. They were standing on a pebble-strewn path in the merchant's garden as they talked, and the moneylender stooped down to pick up the two pebbles. As he did, the girl, sharp-eyed with fright, noticed that he picked up two black pebbles and put them into the money bag. (He wasn't taking any chances.) He then asked the girl to pick out the pebble that was to decide her fate and that of her father.

Imagine that you are standing on that path in the merchant's garden. What would you have done if you had been the girl? If you had to advise her, what would you have advised her to do? What type of thinking would you use to solve the problem? You may think that careful, logical analysis must solve the problem if there is a solution. This type of thinking is straightforward vertical thinking. The other type of thinking is lateral thinking.

Vertical thinkers are usually not much help to a girl in this situation. If you were to examine the way they would analyze it, there are three possibilities: (1) The girl should refuse to take a pebble. (2) The girl should show that there are two black pebbles in the bag and expose the moneylender as a cheat. (3) The girl should take a black pebble and sacrifice herself in order to save her father from prison.

None of these suggestions is very helpful, for if the girl does take a pebble, then she has to marry the moneylender. If not, her father goes to prison.

The girl in the story put her hand into the money bag and drew out a pebble. Without looking at it, she fumbled and let it fall to the path where it was immediately lost among all the others. "Oh, how clumsy of me," she said. "But never mind, if you look into the bag, you will be able to tell which pebble I took by the color of the one that is remaining."

Since the remaining pebble is, of course, black, it must be assumed that she has taken the white pebble, since the moneylender dare not admit his dishonesty.

That's what's called lateral thinking. It not only solves problems, but it also improves the situation.

It is a well-established yet always surprising bit of knowledge that the answer to even our most pressing problem (provided, of course, that it lies within the realm of human solution) is usually at hand. It requires, however, a different kind of insight to see it.

It's like the old story of the big truck that was stuck in an underpass. They didn't know what to do until a youngster, observing their perplexity, suggested that they let some of the air out of the tires. It was a perfectly simple, obvious solution to a tough problem. But it takes a different kind of thinking—it takes lateral thinking, thinking in new directions. Someone once said that thinking in new directions is the definition of genius.

This kind of thinking characteristically produces simple answers. They're the kind that usually trigger the response, "Why didn't I think of that?" or "The answer was so obvious." It's obvious only after someone else comes up with it.

A friend of mine loves to lie on the beach and soak up the sun with a good book. She likes to listen to the radio at the same time. And on receiving a very good little portable for Christmas one year, she was worried about getting sand in it and its being ruined. Her eleven-year-old son suggested that she put it in a plastic bag and fasten the top. It would be sand-proof, yet it could still be dialed, tuned, and heard through the thin plastic.

These are small, relatively unimportant things, but big, vital, and very critical problems can be solved the same way. It's been said that the solution to every problem is so close that you can reach out and touch it. But you can't touch it with your hand until you touch it with a bit of lateral creative thinking.

Children seem to be better at lateral thinking than grownups, unless grownups work at it, practice it. And then they can learn the knack—or perhaps *relearn* it would be more appropriate. We all were highly creative children at one time, before we had it worn off or knocked out of us by unimaginative, dull adults.

The management of a large electronics firm had struggled for months with a production problem that resisted all their efforts to solve it. There were nine women working on that particular assembly line, and finally, in desperation, the management people asked their help in solving the problem. They solved it in a week and in so doing greatly reduced the cost of producing the product. They had been producing it the old way because that's what they had been told to do. They hadn't been asked to do it the best way they could think of.

Go to work on your problems in the same way if you're in a problem-solving kind of work. (If you're not in a problem-solving kind of work, you're unemployed.)

I understand that it's particularly difficult for professional people to think creatively and laterally. It's because they have been so thoroughly conditioned by their education. They've always been told what to do, and they've been told how it's always been done. And they were never asked how to do it better.

How to Brainstorm

WHAT ARE THE SIMILARITIES in problem-solving, decision-making, and goal achievement?

Actually, they're alike in many ways. A decision that must be made is little more than a problem awaiting a solution. We might even call it a simple problem. When we're faced with a decision, we rarely have to choose between more than two or three alternatives, whereas in solving a problem, we sometimes face what seems to be an endless list of possibilities. And what about goal achievement? Isn't a goal a point we wish to reach? The problem is to move from where we are now to where we want to be. So, you see, problem-solving, decision-making, and goal achievement are all closely related functions of creative thinking. It's important that we keep this in mind.

The first step in solving any problem is to define it. We should always be sure we understand a problem before we go to work on its solution.

Next, you should write down everything you know about the problem. This information might come from your own experience; or from books, which contain background and statistical data; or from friends and business associates who know something about the area in which the problem lies.

Third, decide whom to see. List the names of people and organizations that are recognized authorities on the problem. This is your opportunity to go all out for facts. After determining who can help you, contact them, talk with them, and pick their brains for all the information they possess that can help you solve the problem.

After doing this, be sure to make a note of each thing that's germane to the problem. Don't risk forgetting anything that could help you find the best solution.

The fifth step in solving a problem creatively is called individual ideation. This is personal brainstorming, or thinking with the brakes of judgment off. Don't try to decide whether an idea is good or bad; just write it down the moment it comes to you. You can pick and choose, rate these ideas, later. Right now, all you're after is a lot of ideas.

Remember the four rules for brainstorming: (1) no negative thinking; (2) the wilder the ideas, the better; (3) a large number of ideas is essential; and (4) combination and improvement of ideas are what you're after.

One idea often leads to another, better idea. Don't worry if some of your ideas seem far-fetched or impractical. You're looking for all the ideas you can possibly find. Don't reject any. Write them all down!

Then group brainstorm. This is your opportunity to put the minds of others to work on the problem. Handle this session the same way you did your individual ideation. No negative thinking, no criticism at this stage; the wilder the ideas the better. Get as many ideas as possible, and try for idea combination and improvement. Write down all the ideas the group comes up with.

When you have all your ideas written down, rate them for effectiveness and facility. The effectiveness scale ranges from "very effective" to "probably effective" to "doubtful." And the facility scale ranges from "easy" to "not so easy" to "difficult." This rating of ideas will clearly indicate the likely success of any possible solution. Of course, it's best to consider first the idea or ideas that are rated both "very effective" and "easy."

Suppose you're a manufacturer. And suppose your sales and marketing team brainstorm comes up with some ideas to increase sales. Let's say one of the ideas is to revamp completely one of the products that your company is offering to the public. Let's rate this idea in terms of effectiveness. You know the present product meets a need and is acceptable to the buying public. What about an entirely changed product? Without a lot of marketing tests and then a period of actual manufacturing for sale, it would be hard to say just how effective this idea would be in increasing sales. Better rate it "doubtful."

And how does this idea of completely revamping one of the products check out in the facility area—"easy," "not so easy," or "difficult"? It would be "difficult," wouldn't it? It would require new engineering, new tools, new manufacturing plans, new packaging, and new marketing methods.

Suppose, however, that one of the salesmen's ideas is to feature the company's product on a network television program. This would be "probably effective." It would be "not so easy," but it could be done.

Let's say another idea is to set up a new motivational or sales incentive program, a program directed to those people who are at the front of the problem—the salesmen. If it were a well-designed and implemented motivational or incentive program, it would stand a good chance of being "very effective." It would be "easy" to do. It should increase the company sales.

There are many other evaluation yardsticks you might use. Two more are time and money. Try rating your ideas against these measurements. For example, in the case of a manufacturer who wants to increase his sales, certainly to change the product would take a great deal of time and money. And to advertise it on a popular network television program would cost a great deal of money. On the other hand, to introduce a new motivational or sales incentive program might be neither too costly nor too time consuming.

Remember, when you evaluate your ideas, measure them against these four rating yardsticks: effectiveness, facility, time, and cost. Every idea you have may not be worth creative action, and that's why you must skillfully evaluate each of them. But once you've carefully judged your ideas, it's time to take action.

When you've written an idea into your action plan, decide who might do it, when it might be done, whether to start, and how to do it. These are important considerations.

Be certain to give yourself a deadline for putting your plan into action. We work hardest and most efficiently when we know there's a definite time element involved. So, make a note of the date when you must put your solution to work. It's good to remember that timing is often critical when a new idea is introduced. Carefully calculate the deadline in light of the general situation. You also might like to write down a second date—the one by which you intend to have the action completed and the problem solved.

Remember what was said earlier about problem-solving, decision-making, and goal achievement? They have a great deal in common. They can all be attacked in much the same way.

You know, for any problem, no matter how big or complex it may be, there is a solution. All you have to do is find it!

The Power of Our Intuitive Force

WHEN WE THINK long and hard on a problem with an open and receptive consciousness, we put to work energies and forces about which we can only speculate. Most of us have stewed over a difficult problem for weeks when suddenly, during a period of relaxation, the answer to the problem appears—complete, simple, and beautiful—before us.

Dr. Willis Harman gave a talk about a friend of his, the president of a high-tech company who, together with his scientific staff, had been trying to solve an especially knotty problem for weeks. One Sunday afternoon, while he was sitting in his living room, as Dr. Harman recalled he was once again puzzling over the fact that he didn't have anybody in the organization who could solve this technical problem, when he heard a voice say, "Well, what about this?" And there drifted into the living room a three-dimensional model that just sat there which embodied the technological advance that he needed.

He got his pad and pencil and started to sketch it, and when he'd finished the sketch of the front view, it turned around so he could sketch the side view. After he finished that, it flipped over so he could get a top view.

He took his completed sketch into his office and showed it to his top design engineer, who asked him where the idea came from. He very reluctantly told him about the episode in his living room. The engineer broke into a broad grin and said, "That's where I get all of my ideas."

Earlier, in the same talk, Dr. Harman had told of an architect who used the same mysterious source for his best building designs. He'd feed all the necessary information into his mind, stew about the project for a few days, and then, at some odd time, the finished sketches would appear so clearly in every detail, he had only to copy them. One time the idea he was waiting for appeared in front of him on the windshield while he was driving his car.

Dr. Harman calls this strange source of answers the "creative, intuitive deep mind." Those who don't believe in it can't use it. By not believing in it, they've shut off the means of reaching it. Those who believe in it a little tend to use it a little. Those who believe in it a great deal use it all the time.

In science, we know that just about all the great advances were made by these kinds of intuitive leaps in the creative process—by some sort of remarkable solving of problems behind the scenes.

Most people find the system working when they try to remember someone's name. The more they try to force the forgotten name into their consciousness, the more it remains hidden. So they drop it and turn to other things, and after a while, when they're relaxed and doing something else, the name they were looking for floats into their consciousness.

Most people don't realize that the same system that will dredge up a forgotten name will dredge up practically anything else they happen to want or need.

I've used this creative source for answers all my life. Call it collective intuition, call it the subconscious—call it anything at all. But call it. Use it. Believe in it.

YOUR GREATEST ASSET

Remember these steps for brainstorming:

define the problem;

write down everything you know about the problem;

decide whom to see;

make note of everything that's germane to the problem;

conduct a personal brainstorming or individual ideation session;

consider group brainstorming;

rate your ideas for effectiveness, facility, time, and money;

evaluate your ideas and take action on them;

create an action plan;

and give yourself a deadline for putting your plan into action.

How to Build Your Imagination

WHILE GETTING NEW IDEAS in business is usually the best way to guarantee unpopularity, it's still the only way to renewal and growth. People resist new ideas, from the top to the bottom of an organization, especially if it's an older organization. Championing a new idea is a lonely business. But if you believe it's a good idea, if your research causes you to believe it will be a significant benefit, and the costs and disruption necessary to test the idea are not completely out of line with its ultimate benefit, then fight it through. Do it as diplomatically as you can, make as few enemies as possible, but fight it through if you believe in it.

People historically have stood in the way of virtually every good idea, especially if it isn't theirs. Your good ideas can lead to your dismissal from an organization. But ideas are more important than a job. With good ideas you have independence. There's always a way to succeed. A friend of mine found he couldn't get his ideas through the board of directors. He resigned, and beginning at about the age of sixty, he built a three hundred million-dollar-a-year business on his rejected ideas. Walt Disney used to ask ten people what they thought of a new idea. If they were unanimous in their rejection of it, he would begin working on it immediately.

Our world today consists of thousands of things people once thought were impossible. How many good ideas have you followed through to completion in your work during the past year? A business's very beginning and success were based on innovative imagination and will become a model of stodgy convention with a few years of good profits. You know, Arnold Palmer's success as a truly great golfer was based on his ability to never try to play the game too safely. He was never foolhardy, but he would try the more testing shot when others would have played it safe. He lost some tournaments as a result, but he won a great many and achieved world fame and respect, too.

There's much to be said for the conservation of assets. But it should be remembered that they tend to slow you down and put more emphasis on saving what you've got than on building for the future. And of course, there's a happy balance between conservation and innovation that should never be lost sight of.

When it comes to input, we should never stop building our store of information. We can never get an idea without new material, which is information and application. If there's real talent there too, so much the better. But talent has a way of developing with hard application, daily application, perspiration, long hours of study, and deep thought. Become a sponge for information that applies to what you do. Read everything you can find on the subject. Build a fine library of books that are filled with the ideas of others on your specialty—whatever it may be.

You know, each of us has a gold mine between our ears. If you fail to mine the gold, well, that's your business. But it's there—all that we can want and much more.

Learn to Create, Not Compete

SOME TIME AGO, I made a speech to the members of a large national organization. These people were executives at or near the top of the companies they represented. I told them that in my opinion, none of us thinks enough; as a rule, we let our minds lie dormant, sort of in neutral, until we're confronted with a situation that requires mental effort.

I mentioned that even corporation presidents of my acquaintance seldom indulge in serious, concentrated thinking between problems. They think in times of crisis. The fact that they can solve problems and steer their companies safely through crises qualifies them as executives and justifies their large incomes. But what about all that time they have between problems? Why not have some sort of systematic daily plan of creative thinking?

An intelligent person works out some program of physical exercise for the proper maintenance of his body. Why not a daily program of mental exercise?

I know of a lumber dealer in New York who became an outstanding success in a surprisingly short time. He made millions in the lumber business while his so-called competitors were scrambling around, trying to keep up with him.

When reporters asked him the secret of his success, he told them that every night he sat quietly all by himself in a darkened room. During this time, he simply meditated, trying to imagine how the lumber business would be conducted ten years from then. He would jot down the ideas that came to him and then tried to put them into effect in his business at once, instead of waiting for the ten years to pass. In this way, while his contemporaries were competing with each other, he was always creating.

His secret? Never compete; create. Makes sense, doesn't it?

A psychiatrist who was addressing a group of his distinguished colleagues got a big laugh from the audience with this description of the modern executive: "There are four types of executives: first, there's the ulceroidal type, who worries about the problem; second, there's the thyroidal type, who runs around the problem; third, there's the adenoidal type, who screams and yells about it; and fourth, there's the hemorrhoidal type, who sits on it and waits for everything to clear up."

Every adult is an executive, if not of the company he works for, at least of his own life and his family. What kind of an executive are you? Are you creating, or are you competing?

Why not try each day to do some concentrated, independent thinking about yourself, your life, and the people you serve? I think you will agree with me that anything, however good, can be improved.

Henry Ford said, "Thinking is the hardest work there is, which is the probable reason why so few engage in it."

YOUR GREATEST ASSET

Make a deal with yourself to set aside one hour each night for creative thought.

Instead of worrying about the competition, try forecasting new paths for growth in your life. Be sure to examine:

your job,

your company,

your personal relationships.

What new ideas can you think of?

Developing Your Creative Mind

YOU MIGHT WANT TO THINK about this trenchant statement: "Thus the materials for the creative product lie all about us, equally accessible to everyone. What keeps us from being more creative is a frame of mind...that persists in seeing only the commonplace in the familiar. We become frozen in the ice of our conservatism, and the world congeals about us."

Care to think about that for a year or two? A tremendous, devastating, magnificent indictment. I've said before that every day of our lives every one of us walks by more creative opportunity than he could probably effectively develop in a lifetime. There is no situation that is not charged with possibilities.

There are possibilities for creativity in the things by which we're surrounded in our daily work in the home, in all the rooms of the home, in the yard or garden, on the drive or commute to and from work, in the daily newspaper, the radio and television (not necessarily in that order, by any means). In the clothes we wear, the houses we pass, and the empty lots. In everything we do, with every waking moment of every day, 365 days a year, we are face to face with an abundant supply of the materials of creativity. But it takes that "state of mind," that sense of ambient opportunity, of the nearness and the excitement of a possibility-charged existence. Otherwise, we "persist in seeing only the commonplace in the familiar. We become frozen in the ice of our [own] conservatism, and the world congeals [around] us."

There is no security in life. Why do we try to play it safe? We eat and wear and are sheltered by what we have produced. If, through the great lever of our imagination and latent creative ability, we can make a more significant contribution from the spot on which we stand, there is perhaps much to gain and very little to lose. Besides, we certainly don't have to stop with one attempt!

I remember the comment of the well-known motion-picture producer, Mike Todd: "Being broke is a temporary situation, being poor is a state of mind."

We can say that creativity is a state of mind as well. It's a state of mind that typifies the very young because of the newness of the world. In time, through social pressures to conform and the repetition of experience, most children lose this sense of wonder and become less and less creative, trapped in a concrete mold not of their own making.

It's been said that the creative person is essentially a perpetual child. The tragedy seems to be that most of us grow up.

YOUR GREATEST ASSET

How to Gain the Most from Creative Thinking

When you ask yourself why the steering wheel on your car is round, it's not necessarily because you want to invent a square one; it's because you're practicing your art—the art of creative thinking.

MOST PEOPLE TODAY agree that the once fervently spoken line, "What was good enough for my father is good enough for me," was a fatuous, absurd remark. What was good enough for Dad is not good enough for us today, and what's good enough for us won't be good enough for our youngsters. That's the way this old world improves itself, and that's the way it should be.

A leading businessman has said, "If you're doing anything this year the same way you did it last year—you're in serious trouble." The trouble might not come from the way you're doing things, but it very likely will come unless you maintain a constant awareness of the necessity—the inevitability—of change.

Creative thinking is a learnable skill and a practical art. But creative thinking, by the very nature, resists perfect definition and rigid rules of conduct, as does music or paint or any other art.

Becoming accomplished at any art takes practice and more practice—years of it. You can start practicing it right now; you can make it one of your most valuable assets now and from here on out. And if you'll continue to practice every day of your life, you'll become a master at it and win a master's rewards.

Maybe it doesn't make any difference if you still lace your shoes the way you have always laced them, but it does make a difference if you don't challenge the way you lace them or why you lace them. Just such a challenge changed the shoe industry, and today a good many men's shoes are made with no laces at all.

So, form the habit of really thinking about, of questioning, everything you do, everything you see. Some people can walk by an empty lot for years without giving it a second thought, without really seeing it at all. But one man will see it, not as a vacant lot, but as a beautifully landscaped property sporting a handsome new office building. He'll do something worthwhile for his community and probably make himself a fine profit in real estate.

When you ask yourself why the steering wheel on your car is round, it's not necessarily because you want to invent a square one; it's because you're practicing your art—the art of creative thinking. You're sharpening your mind and encouraging it to perform the highest function a human being is capable of—deliberate, creative thought.

Then, when you apply your art to your work, to your home and family and friends—your mind flashes out of its scabbard like a finely tempered steel blade—probing, seeking, penetrating through the old to the new that lies just under the surface.

Creative thinking is an exciting pursuit; it's exhilarating, and it makes for wonderful conversation at the dinner table, while riding in the car, at any time. In the evening, your creative awareness might result in your asking yourself, "Why am I sitting here like a mesmerized chicken watching people kill each other from the backs of homes on my television screen? Isn't there something more interesting, more rewarding, I could be doing with a part of this time? Isn't there a subject I would like to know more about? What about that book I've been meaning to read?"

You know, one hour a night adds up quickly to a really enormous amount of time. Time is one of the few things man can't buy more of, and it's a good idea to use all of it as wisely as we know how.

When you get an idea that you think is good, hang it up on an imaginary hook and walk all the way around it. Look at it from every angle, poke it, pull it, twist it. Stretch it in new directions. Try to improve it. If it's an idea you can't use, give it away and get another you can work with. Ideas are free, yet they're the most valuable commodities known to man. And great ideas enable the minds that conceive them.

Make creative thinking a normal part of your life and attitude, and you'll find your world being filled to the brim with wonderful new interest. And one of these days, you're going to get the idea that will make a really substantial contribution—one that will revolutionize your life! For it will be an idea that will make the world a better place because you happened to live here for a while.

In the meantime, just looking for that idea can be a challenge, an inspiration, and a lot of fun!

Good hunting and good creative thinking!

Chapter Seven

How to Be a Master at Public Speaking

They Laughed When I Stood Up to Talk

ARE YOU NERVOUS or just plain scared when it comes to standing up on your feet and talking to a group of people? It seems that millions are. It used to terrify me, as a matter of fact. I remember years ago in Los Angeles I was to make a talk before six thousand people in the Shrine Auditorium. I hadn't done a great deal of public speaking before then, and I remember walking up and down the street outside the stage door in a sweat verging on pure panic for an hour before the time arrived. When I finally walked out on the stage before so many thousands of people, I was in a kind of walking coma. Once I got started, it was alright, but the anticipation was pure torture. It doesn't bother me like that anymore, although I still get the ubiquitous butterflies in the stomach.

My friend Norm Guess, formerly of the Dartnell Company in Chicago, sent me a little piece on some of the causes of our fear of groups:

1. **The fear of self.** Just plain self-consciousness, a feeling that expresses itself in the mental question, "What in blazes am I doing this for? How in the world did I get into this situation?"

2. **Reflections from the past.** The remembrance, even subliminally, of old classroom failures, being laughed at or ridiculed.

3. **Overconcern about what others think.** The questioning of our authority to be talking before such a group.

4. **Poor preparation.** The panicky feeling that the speech needs work, complete overhauling, or throwing away.

5. **Lack of courage to try new things.** The fear of doing the unusual.

6. **Lack of encouragement from others.** I know it always helps me tremendously to hear a comment such as, "The group is looking forward to hearing what you have to say.

7. **The place itself.** The room can be arranged wrong. Too few people in too large a room. And the worst thing of all, as far as I'm concerned, is a five-and-dime public address system that sounds

bad, or one of those little microphones you have to practically swallow, or a stand mike front of the podium that you have to reach around with both arms to work with your notes. One night the equipment was so bad I just quit talking and told the chairman of the meeting that his organization should invest in some good equipment before they invited people to speak to them.

Well, what do you do about these problems?

1. Recognize that others have the same fears.
2. Try to analyze what and why you fear.
3. Find a compulsion to speak; realize that you have important things to say and that you want to say them.
4. Be prepared.
5. Try to practice participation when in small groups.
6. Take notes. Writing ideas down helps so much.
7. If it's absolutely crucial, practice beforehand.
8. Learn to counter fear before a meeting begins. That takes time and practice.
9. You can take a course. Join Toastmasters; it's a great organization full of people you'd like to know anyway.
10. There's nothing like actually doing it. Do it.

And my personal admonition is to talk only on a subject you know very well—something you're an expert on and feel comfortable with.

Someone has said, "The human mind is a wonderful thing. It begins at birth and never stops until you get the chance to say something before a group of people." Turn the situation around; realize that if you were in the audience, you'd be interested in what you have to say.

The Most Important Element in a Speech

That's the secret: be interesting. If you can't be interesting, shut up. There's nothing wrong with silence.

"WHAT IS THE SINGLE MOST important element necessary to make an effective speech?" I don't think that's a difficult question at all.

The most important element necessary to make an effective speech is to be interesting. If you cannot make what you have to say interesting, you shouldn't be making a speech in the first place.

Some say the one vital ingredient is enthusiasm. I don't agree. I've heard many speakers who were extremely enthusiastic about their subjects and left me completely bored. I agree that it's good to be enthusiastic about your subject, and if it's interesting, you should be...and so will the audience.

The one ingredient vital to selling anything—education, religion, hope, marriage, a product or service—is to be interesting. Unless you have the person's interest, you're simply not going to really reach him or move him to make some kind of commitment.

I remember the story about the little boy who came crying to his father with the news that his turtle had died. His father looked at the recumbent creature in his son's hand and thought fast. "I know," he said, "we'll invite some of your friends over and we'll have a big funeral. We'll dig a little grave in the backyard and make a little coffin, and we'll have a parade. I'll speak some words over dead Herkimer there and..." And about that time, the father noticed that the turtle was moving. "Hey son, look! Your turtle isn't dead after all!"

The boy looked at the now animated creature, then looked at his dad with a sly grin and said, "Let's kill him!"

The father had been such a great salesman in selling his son the benefits of a funeral with all the trappings...it now loomed larger and more interesting to the boy than the survival of his pet turtle. And that's the secret: be interesting. If you can't be interesting, shut up. There's nothing wrong with silence.

The secret to being interesting, if you don't have the natural talent of the little boy's father in our story, is to plan what you have to say. Even in conversation you can take a moment or two to arrange your words and the way you say something so as to make it more interesting. But that's the key—it's the most important factor in selling anything. And we're all selling something all the time.

Our responsibility in attempting to get others to do things we want them to do is to be interesting. A little thought, a little planning, will usually do the trick.

How to Make a Speech

HAVE YOU EVER BEEN ASKED to make a speech? There are two kinds of public speakers: there are those who are asked to talk to a group, and there are those who, because of their position, are forced to talk before groups—people such as ministers, teachers, executives, and sales managers.

In the first instance—that is, if you're asked to make a speech—it means you know something others want to hear. It usually means you're an expert on some subject. If you're not an expert on the subject, don't accept the invitation to make the speech. If you do accept and have before you the prospect of standing alone in front of a crowd of people, you have quite a responsibility.

The person whose job demands that he talk before groups has an even greater responsibility. In the first case, people come because they want to; in the second case, they have to listen to you whether they like it or not.

But in either case, you can make a good speech with a little preparation. Here are some guidelines:

The first thing to understand is that if it's your first speech, you're going to be scared. You'll find a dull, leaden dread begin to build up within you as the fateful day approaches. Finally, as you're being introduced, you'll come close to panic. This is perfectly normal and happens to just about everyone—and it doesn't stop after the first speech, either. You'll find yourself trembling (particularly at the knees), your hands will perspire, your mouth will become dry, and you'll feel like you're in the terminal stages of some kind of tropical fever. Don't worry about it—just stand up, smile, and begin!

Now, about the preparation of your speech. Write it out completely—this is the way I suggest that you do it. This is a particularly good idea if you've never made one before. Start with an interesting statement that will capture your audience's attention, state your case, give them enough corroborative facts to prove your case, summarize what you've said, bring it to a close, and then sit down. One of the dangers of making a speech is that our voice sounds so good to us after a while that we start believing it sounds just as good to everyone else. This is not necessarily true. It's a thousand times better to quit too soon than to talk for five minutes longer than you should. Besides, you should finish with your audience still interested and wanting more. Don't talk until they're bored.

Don't ever tell jokes. This is one of the worst mistakes most public speakers make. Unless you're a real comedian—unless you're a genuinely funny person—don't enter one of the most difficult fields in the world, the field of a comedian. If you can tell a humorous incident that ties in with what you're talking about, fine. But don't ever, as long as you live, say, "This reminds me of a story..." and so on. The only person worse than the one who tells jokes is the fool who tells off-color jokes.

I make it a principle always to arrive for a speech early so that I can talk to the officials of the group. I find out what the people do and their general education background to make sure they're square with what I had believed when I had prepared my talk. What's the average age? The idea is to know your audience as well as possible so that you can speak to the people in it in their language.

You will remember that when Bob Hope made his hundreds of appearances before servicemen and women all over the world, he would go to some pains to pick up some of their vocabulary and the names of some of their officers. In that way, he could personalize his performance to that particular unit. Well, we should do the same thing without becoming too cute or personal. We just want them to know that we've gone to the trouble to do some research and that we know to whom we're talking—that we're not delivering a canned speech without consideration for the people who must sit through it.

Almost anyone can make a good speech. Just be sure you're talking on a subject you know thoroughly and in which you're deeply interested. Say what you want to say as best you can. Avoid clichés. Never say, "As you know..." If they already know it, you don't have to say it. Tell them what you know in a heartfelt and interesting manner. Become so interested in what you're talking about that you can forget yourself; in a way, you'll lose your self-consciousness. And then sit down. That's all there is to it.

YOUR GREATEST ASSET

Remember these steps for a good speech:

Accept that you'll be nervous.

Write out a speech that's concise, interesting, and that proceeds in a logical order.

Don't tell jokes, and avoid clichés.

Arrive early to learn about your audience.

Become so interested in your subject that you forget yourself.

The Single-Theme Formula

PROFESSIONAL SALESPEOPLE, marketing experts, and leaders in the advertising profession know the importance of selling one thing a time. Only catalogs can successfully handle a multitude of items. In a five-minute speech or even a long speech, I think it's important to have a single theme and, like a good salesperson, you pose the problem and then give your solution. At the end, the problem is restated and the solution quickly summarized.

Your opening statement should be an attention getter. For example, you might say, "Scientists all over the world agree that the world's oceans are dying"—a sobering thought indeed. It captures immediate interest, and everyone is thinking, "Why, that would presage the end of the world. What are we doing about it?"

Using an internationally recognized authority as your reference, someone such as Jacques Cousteau, you provide the supporting evidence that your opening remark is indeed true, and then you proceed to outline the possible ways that the disaster might be averted. At the end, you might say, "Yes, the oceans of the world are dying today, but if we can marshal the combined efforts of the world's peoples, if we can influence every maritime country to pass laws governing the pollution of the seas by oil tankers..." So you end on a note of hope and at the same time enlist the sympathy of every one of your listeners in your cause.

Not all talks are about social problems, of course—you might be talking about a recent fishing trip, for example—in which case you find something of special interest in the story and open with that. You might say, "Ounce for ounce, the rainbow trout is one of the gamiest fish on earth." It's a much better attention getter and interest stimulator than saying, "I want to tell you about my recent fishing trip." A few words about the fish you were after and then you can work in the rest. "Two weeks ago, John Cooper and I decided to try our luck on the White River near Carter, Arkansas. It's one of the most naturally beautiful spots in the country" and so on. Stay with the trip and that rainbow trout, the hero of your story, and how good it tasted cooked over an open fire on the bank of the river. Then at close, to more closely link your listeners to the subject, you might say, "If you've never been trout fishing, let me recommend it as one of the world's best ways to forget your problems, clear your brain, and gain a new perspective. And when you hook a rainbow trout, you're in for one of the greatest thrills of a lifetime."

Watch your personal pronouns. Keep yourself out of your conversation as much as possible. As with the case of the fishing story, talk about the fish, the beautiful scenery, and your companions, other people you met, a humorous incident or two perhaps, but don't keep saying, "I did this and I did that." The purpose of the speech is not to talk about you but rather the subject matter. There's an old saying that small minds talk about things, average minds talk about people, and great minds talk about ideas. What you're selling is almost always a good idea, even if it's painting the house. The idea is the good appearance or the protection of the house. The fishing trip story is about the idea of getting away and going after exciting game fish. One idea, well developed, is the key.

If you're talking about a long trip you've made, the idea is the trip itself, even though your talk may include many interesting and unusual events and sites along the way. It's still one theme, just as a beautiful painting is put together by a thousand brush strokes. Each stroke makes a contribution to the main theme, the overall picture. And it's the same with a good speech.

The difference, I think, between a memorable speech and an ordinary one is usually the degree of involvement on the part of the speaker. If he's wrapped up in his subject and he knows what he's talking about and he's personally involved in it, that comes through. It's not in the words he uses; it's in the feeling that's transmitted. If you want to test this out, listen to the news broadcasts on your radio or watch them on television. The performer who's only reading the news from a script or teleprompter, who has no real knowledge or personal interest in it, tends to be superficial or generally dull.

The reporter who's been there, who's live on the news, who's made the collection and dissemination of news his lifework, brings conviction and interest, involvement you and I are caught up in. We simply know that he knows what he's talking about, while the other person is only reading. It's the same when giving a speech. If the person telling the story about the fishing trip is an avid fisherman and loves it, it comes through. So try to talk about things in which you're very interested. And use the single theme formula. It makes preparing a talk much easier and the delivering of it much more effective.

On Writing a Speech

The ideas are the important thing. If you're successful in getting the ideas across from your mind to the minds of your audience, you're as successful as a speaker is supposed to be. Audiences have a way of knowing when you're more interested in what you're saying than in how you appear.

THE PERSON WHO DOES a lot of speaking will usually have a fine library and be a good reader and have a good working knowledge of his language. If you're writing a speech and you're not sure of your grammar, especially syntax, have a person who's more knowledgeable on the language edit it for you. You might brush up a little bit too.

If you're at all unsure of a word's pronunciation, by all means, look it up and check it carefully. Mispronounced words drop like bombs into an audience.

Sloppy speech habits must go if we're to stand up and speak to an audience. We owe it to them. It's offensive otherwise.

It's very difficult to write and speak flawless English, of course, but we can do the best we are capable of and pursue the subject on a regular basis. I think I own about 150 books on the English language, on writing, and so on. I think a speaker has a responsibility to set a good example when he speaks. If he can't do that, he should remain in the audience.

The exception would be the entertainer who depends on homespun colloquialisms for a part of his humor. When I was with CBS many years ago, I once interviewed a well-known newspaper columnist. I was amazed to hear him mispronouncing words I'd read in his columns. Then it dawned on me that he was print-oriented. He knew the words well and their meanings and used them regularly in his writing, but they weren't in his speech vocabulary. I remember that he mispronounced the word "indisputable." He said "indispute-able," and there were a sprinkling of other mispronunciations.

It's a good idea not to use words in your speech that you're not accustomed to in your ordinary speech, unless you're sure of their pronunciation.

Now we come to the critical part—no more critical than the writing, of course, but certainly of equal import. Read what you've written. Unless you're an expert at it, and few are, I suggest you read it over numerous times. Now this, of course, is for the speech that must be letter perfect. As you do, you'll always find ways of smoothing it out, adding a bit here, deleting something there. When the time comes to present your speech, you'll be intimately acquainted with its every word and nuance. Remember to keep your sentences very short. When you look at a sentence or even a short paragraph, you'll quickly grasp its meaning and intent.

Don't be too concerned about how great you look. The ideas are the important thing. If you're successful in getting the ideas across from your mind to the minds of your audience, you're as successful as a speaker is supposed to be. Audiences have a way of knowing when you're more interested in what you're saying than in how you appear. No phony gestures or posturing. When the gestures come, they're genuine and everybody knows it. The good speaker is like the good salesman who's more interested in how great his product is and in helping the customer than in his commission check.

Or the fine actor who so loses himself in his part that the character he's playing takes the stage and the actor usually disappears. You've heard it said of some actors that no matter what part they're playing, they're still themselves.

Well, it's the same with speakers. Few of them have enough interest in what they're saying and in the audience to forget themselves.

For practice in writing your own speeches, I recommend that you simply start writing them. Write two or three speeches, and see how they come out. Remember to keep your sentences very short so you can breathe in the right places. And keep your copy lean and muscular. Cut out superfluous words and clichés. Get to the point. Stay with the point. And do a wrap up. Find something interesting for the close and sit down. We learn to write well by writing, by sitting down and making little black marks on paper. The more we do it, the better we get at it, as it is with anything else.

A Good Speech Is Like Good Conversation

A GOOD CONVERSATIONALIST will make a good speaker. He's sensitive to the presence of others. His antennae are forever alert, picking up signals from his audience and involving them in his talk.

Good conversation is one of the great joys of human commerce. Good conversation should be like the game of tennis, in which the ball is struck back and forth with each player participating equally. Bores are like golfers who just keep hitting their own ball, over and over and over again.

A good conversationalist is one who, after he's held the floor for a minute or so, or has completed saying something he wanted to say, will end with a well-phrased and directed question, involving another player in the game. He will see to it that the conversation shifts from him to someone else. That is a good conversationalist. And they are so rare that they could hold their annual convention in the back seat of a compact car. We love such people. They're a joy to be around.

All right. What does that have to do with making a speech? Well, it has a good deal to do with it.

The good speaker is able to achieve a marvelous give-and-take with his audience, just as a good conversationalist does with the person he's with.

He talks with the audience without their having to say a word. As his audience asks questions such as, "Do you agree with that?"

he'll pause and watch for clues, for evidence that they either do or do not agree with what he's said. Now that's a form of conversation.

Well, the audience can talk to us, too, by their silence, by their attention, by their nods and their poking of the person sitting next to them, and also by their laughter and by their seriousness at the right places.

We've mentioned that people in our society desire recognition more than any other factor. Pausing for a response of the kind I've mentioned here is a form of recognition. It's looking at your audience. It's really seeing them. It's asking them questions and waiting a moment for a response of some kind.

If they're bored, they'll find ways of showing it, despite their best efforts. If they're interested, they'll show that too.

And when we ask a question, they'll respond. That's why the seminar approach is so interesting and often welcomed by the participants. It involves the audience in a very literal and vocal way. A seminar involves a smaller number of people, usually, and asks for their actual participation in the subject under discussion.

I rather imagine that a good conversationalist will make a good speaker. He's sensitive to the presence of others. His antennae are forever alert, picking up signals from his audience and involving them in his talk. The bore will also bore an audience. He'll keep hammering away at the same ball over and over again, totally oblivious to the feelings or negative feedback of his audience. Then he's outraged when people begin falling asleep or talking to each other in the back of the room or sneaking out.

We're free to handle our subject as we will, but freedom does not mean license to impinge on the rights and feelings of others. We have a duty to be interesting or we shouldn't get up in the first place.

Now, that's the task of the speaker, whether he's the manager of the sales force, in a car dealership, an insurance agency, real estate office, or a large international organization. When interest leaves, the sell goes out of his message. Watching and listening for the response of the people we're talking to is a good way to find out how we're doing. It's also the mark of a good conversationalist.

Our responsibility is not only to create a speech that will lead an audience to a believable conclusion; we must also make the very building blocks of that conclusion as fascinating as we can. It is in this way that we can hold the attention of our audience until we get to that all-important final point. In addition, if we can develop techniques that make our audience feel that we are conversing with them, we will convey that we care what they are thinking, and that will create the emotional climate for them to accept us as favorably as possible.

Using Humor

HUMOR ISN'T SOMETHING that can be forced, nor should it be reached for. It's something that almost comes naturally to those with the ability, or at least it seems to.

First, it should be fairly quick. I think it was Will Rogers who said, "Never make the porch too big for the meeting house." By that he meant don't ever make the mistake of spending more time building up a story than the punch line can support. They both should be in a beautiful kind of balance, the kind for which every good humorist has an intuitive feel.

But you know if you're a funny person or not. The knack for humor, I imagine, starts early, as does the reputation for it. I once looked at my autograph book from my high school graduation after thirty years and was amazed to find my friends had written such things as "good luck to our storyteller." It seems that I was getting ready for my years in the broadcast business while still in my teens. Such things appear early. And I'm sure humor does also. If you have it, congratulations. Use it wisely. If you don't have it, use it sparingly and make certain it's really funny before you use it at all.

Does it really tie in with what you say, or are you reaching out into left field to drag it in by the heels? I've heard so many tedious speakers say, following the introduction, "That reminds me of a story..." and then they proceed to tell a story that hasn't the faintest resemblance to anything said in the introduction at all. It didn't remind him. He just wanted to tell a joke, and everybody in the audience knows it and begins to move their feet and cough and look around for the exit.

Why tell it? Jokes aren't necessary to the opening of a speech. Why do a speech at all? Neither are funny comments, unless they have a clever tie-in of some sort that the audience will genuinely appreciate and enjoy.

Here's a good rule to follow that I've found works: If there is any doubt in your mind whatever, if there is the faintest feeling of uneasiness about a story, never tell it. That feeling of uneasiness is your more intelligent subconscious trying to tell you to forget it. Save it for the locker room at the club if you must tell it. Even then, you may see a man you admire turn and walk away.

I don't think we should ever use a so-called joke that in any way insults a member of any minority.

If you want a foolproof system, use the enormously successful Jack Benny system: make yourself the joke. Benny has produced the most prolonged, helpless laughter in the history of show business. It happened on his old radio program when he was approached by a robber who said, "Your money or your life." What followed was simply silence—the deadly, convulsively funny silence that only Jack Benny could manage. The silence lasted only a few seconds when the laughter began, then mounted and mounted and continued for a record-breaking period of time—I think something like fifteen minutes. Finally, when it did subside, the robber repeated, "I said, your money or your life." And Jack Benny replied, "I'm thinking; I'm thinking."

Again the laughter took hold, and the program nearly ran out of time before it could even attempt to finish. A simple silence did it as Jack tried desperately to decide which was more important to him, his money or his life. He was always the loser in his elaborate plans, as is the coyote in his attempts to trap the roadrunner. People love us when we're foiled by our own weaknesses.

The most pitiful person ever to stand before the microphone is the totally tactless person who isn't aware that he's offending his audience and, despite the total lack of laughter at his stories, persists. Fortunately for all of us, he tends to disappear in a short time and is never heard from again.

If humor is your forte, then you don't need any advice or help from me. If it isn't, use it sparingly and in good taste. It's wonderful when it's right. It's so awful when it isn't.

Speaking with Style

I WAS A SPEAKER at a hospital benefit, and as I waited in the wings of a large theater where the benefit was being staged, one of the officials for the evening was on stage in front of the lectern reading the names of the various high school graduates from the community who had won scholarships in nursing. He never looked up at the audience. He spoke in such low monotones that he was difficult to hear, even with an excellent public address system, and his performance was as lackluster as any I've ever seen. When he was through, he walked back to where I was standing in the wings. As he disappeared from view to the audience, his face broke with a beautiful broad smile and he said in a strong voice, "Man, am I glad that's over." I stopped him, and I said, "You should have flashed that wonderful smile to the audience and used your normal voice. It's excellent." "Oh, that," he shuddered. "I'm scared to death out there."

Now, the audience got a picture of a very lackluster man with no personality and no style whatsoever, a total cipher. Yet here was a good-looking man with a beautiful smile, an excellent style of his own that his friends and acquaintances no doubt greatly admired. I wanted to go on stage and say to that great audience, "I wish you could see so-and-so as he really is. He's quite a guy."

Everyone has his or her own special style. It seems to come with the genes and the upbringing and the education, all of thousands of experiences that coalesce to form a person's own unique style.

You have only to study prominent people on television to see quickly that each of them has a style all his own of which he or she is completely unconscious. Just as we should never doubt our hunches or our own unique powers, we should never doubt that we have a natural style. If, and it's a big if—if we can be natural.

It's what made Arthur Godfrey one of the highest paid radio and television salesmen in the business. People loved him because he was just Arthur. The same with Johnny Carson, Perry Como, or the late Bing Crosby and just about every truly successful star in the business. They play themselves when they're on. And you and I should, too.

However—and I think this is also of extreme importance—we need to understand what we might call the star factor. We need to understand the importance of losing ourselves in our subjects. We don't lose control. We know where we are and what we are doing.

Our minds reach for the proper words and phrases, the pauses come in the right places, and we've got good eye contact with our audience. You might say we're conscious of putting on a performance, but at the same time we're so interested in what we're talking about and we know our subject so thoroughly we can immerse ourselves in it.

I was chatting with a salesman on an airplane one time. It turned out we were both going to the same convention. I had to speak. He had to receive his company's highest honor as national sales leader. As our conversation grew more animated, I asked him the secret of being No. 1 in sales with his company. And he gave me the most interesting answer. He said, "I was in this business for several years, and I tried hard and I worked hard, but I was a long way from the top. Then one day, a wonderful thing happened. All of a sudden things were turned around. Instead of my being in this business, the business got into me."

He looked at me, and his eyes were shining; and he asked, "Do you know what I mean?" I told him I knew exactly what he meant and he could number himself among the most fortunate human beings on earth—the people who actually enjoy what they're doing, the real stars.

It reminded me of John Stuart Mills's theory of happiness in his book *Utilitarianism*. He said that those only are happy who do not seek happiness directly but who spend their time helping others, who are engaged in some art or pursuit followed not as a means but as itself an ideal end. Doing something else, they find happiness along the way. The important part is that those are happiest who are daily engaged in a pursuit followed not just as a means but as itself an ideal end. And it's the same in making a fine speech.

Unless the speech is in us to the extent that we can forget ourselves to a degree it will never carry the impelling, moving effect of a great speech, the kind that brings the audience to its feet at the end of it.

I'll never forget as a youngster hearing Franklin D. Roosevelt say in a campaign speech in that high, stentorian, and effective voice, "We must prevent the princes of privilege from dominating this great country." I remember so vividly the beautiful alliteration "prevent the princes of privilege." Alliteration sticks in the mind as does short poetry. At one time earlier in our culture, virtually all oral traditions, passed from one generation to another, were in a kind of poetry because it was easier to remember. How can we ever forget "Mary had a little lamb"; or "Thirty days hath September, April, June, and November"; or "A, B, C, D, E, F, G, H, I, J, K…" Or how about powerful onomatopoeia such as "the stock market hit bottom with an ominous thud?" Well, perhaps I could have thought of a more cheerful example.

But there is poetry in the proper use of words. We hear so many bad speeches; a good one is like a cool green oasis in a burning desert. A good, but unaffected style helps.

On Moderating a Panel

IF YOU'RE ASKED TO VOLUNTEER to handle the job of panel moderator, you're already well acquainted with the topics to be discussed or you have considerable experience in the field about which the meeting has been called. Given your familiarity with the general topics to be discussed and questions that may come from the audience, I would say your second most important job is to familiarize yourself with the backgrounds of the panel members. By doing so, you're in an excellent position to steer questions to the appropriate panel member and to make comments of interest in background material that will prime the pump and give your panel members enthusiastic participation.

If the manager of the meeting appoints or asks you to moderate a panel after the general meeting has arrived at the meeting site, try to spend some time with your panel and make notes that will help you get the meeting started and/or keep it moving in the event that it stalls, which I've seen happen many times. The interest generated in the liveliness of a panel discussion will depend on the moderator, who also assumes the job of master of ceremonies once the meeting is in progress.

If you know you're to moderate a panel well in advance of the meeting, which should be the case, there are some excellent ways to practice the job. For example, bring up subjects of interest and ask the members of your family to tell you when a comment begins to run dry. Switch to another person or bring up another aspect of the subject and direct a question to a specific person. You can do this at business luncheons, too.

The good moderator is one who asks interesting and germane questions and/or can take a poorly phrased question and rephrase it to make it clearer and more interesting. Another good idea is to watch the good panel shows on television, especially those that are news-oriented, such as *Face the Nation* and others that have earned for themselves places of created permanence and excellence.

When you're asked to handle a panel discussion or to field questions from the audience, never forget that your job is to feature your panel members, not to make a speech yourself or in any way dominate a discussion unless the questioner from the audience asks you the question directly. Panels at conventions are there to draw interested audiences. People are there to learn and get answers to their questions. Quite often, a question is much more critical to the inquirer than members of the audience realize.

The moderator should see to it that the questioner receives more than a superficial answer, if one exists, without dwelling too long on any one question. Moderators should be on their guard against notice-seeking or thoughtless people in the audience who attempt to dominate the question process or use the meeting as a forum for their own long-winded views. Such people should be cut off and the audience reminded of the purpose of the sessions. You may need an extrovert or two out there in the audience to get the meeting rolling, but you want to make sure that those with important questions are heard and their questions properly commented upon.

Keep a good casual perspective. Consult the questions in your notes to make sure the most important have been discussed, and keep your sense of humor.

Panel discussions must be unrehearsed and can, therefore, be surprising at times. They're also often terribly dull, which is a sign of a poor moderator or one who has not had time to properly prepare. If you're in charge of a meeting, find your panel members and moderator as far in advance of the meeting as practicable. And in appointing them or finding them, make them aware of the importance of this meeting and that it should be interesting and informative.

> ## YOUR GREATEST ASSET
>
> **What's the role of a good moderator?**
>
> **Have you prepared yourself to keep the discussion interesting and germane to the subject at hand?**
>
> **Are you prepared to keep the discussion moving forward and to maintain a sense of humor?**

Chapter Eight

THE LASTING BENEFITS OF GOOD SERVICE

Why Are We Here?

It's been said, "If the universe is an accident, we are accidents. But if there is meaning in the universe, there is meaning in us also."

How would you answer the question, "Why are you here?" Go ahead, ask the question. Ask, "Why am I here?" Do you know?

Dr. Albert Einstein was asked to answer that question, and he did. Do you know what he said? I'll get to that in a moment.

It's been said, "If the universe is an accident, we are accidents. But if there is meaning in the universe, there is meaning in us also." And since it is believed that Dr. Einstein understood more about the laws governing the universe than any person who ever lived up until his time, let's go to him for some answers. He believed there was some sort of meaning in the way things are. He was sure of it. He said, "The more I study physics, the more I am drawn toward metaphysics." The word *metaphysics* simple means "beyond physics"; the study of what is beyond measure, the invisible forces at work.

If you haven't done so, you would enjoy reading *Einstein: The Life and Times* by Ronald W. Clark. Albert Einstein was so remarkable a man that it was as if he had arrived on this planet through some mistake in celestial navigation and, as a result, devoted his life to solving the problems of time and space so that the mistake would not be repeated.

Dr. Einstein belonged to no formal religion or sect, yet he was a deeply religious man in the cosmic sense. He believed that such magnificence and colossal order—the great "cyclotron of the universe," as Ronald Clark puts it—could not have been an accident.

And he addressed himself to the purpose of life. He answered the question, "Why am I here?" as well as it has been answered when he said, "Man is here for the sake of other men only." He used the word *man* in its classical sense, the idiomatic "man" meaning human beings of both sexes, of course.

So he said that we are here for the sake of others only. Is that the way you would have answered it? Do you believe that you are here solely to serve others and, through serving others, are being served and enjoying life as a result?

We are here for the sake of serving others only! And to the extent that we serve others will we know the joy of living. To many, that would sound silly and "square," but that's what it comes down to, nevertheless. And sometimes it takes a long time to learn the truth of it. Millions never learn it and grow old in querulous discontent, wondering what went wrong with their lives.

Our Rewards Equal Our Contributions

"OUR REWARDS IN LIFE will always be in direct proportion to our contribution." This is the law that stands as the supporting structure of all economics and of our personal well-being.

Unfortunately, most people either don't know about this wonderful rule or think that somehow it applies only to the other guy. Most people believe that we should have speed-limit signs, too, but that they're for other people who don't know how to drive as well as they do.

Let's get back to the law of rewards equaling contributions. The law is in operation all the time, whether or not we know about it and go along with it. It's like an apothecary's scale—you know the kind, with a cross-arm on top, from which hang two bowls on chains; a delicate and honest mechanism. Let's label one of the bowls "Rewards" and the other one "Contributions."

Most people concentrate on the bowl marked "Rewards." That is, they want things: more money, a better home, education for the kids, travel, retirement, and so on—all rewards. They're hungering for the rewards, but the rewards aren't materializing because they're forgetting the bowl marked "Contributions." In other words, they're concentrating on the wrong bowl. They're like the man who sat in front of the stove and said, "Give me heat, and then I'll give you wood." He could sit there until he froze to death. Stoves don't work that way, and neither does life or economics.

We can actually forget about the bowl marked "Rewards." All we have to do is concentrate on the bowl marked "Contributions." Life and basic economics will automatically take care of the rewards. It's a fact that most people have this backward.

What do we mean by contribution, and to whom do we contribute? You can define contribution as the time you devote to whatever it is you do and the degree of excellence you put into it. And your contribution is to mankind, and mankind can be defined as the people you serve.

So you can break it all down to a simple equation: your rewards will be determined by the way you do your job, multiplied by the number of people you serve.

If a person isn't happy with his rewards, he should take a good, long look at his contributions. This may seem like a hard, cruel way of looking at things, but laws are good or bad only in the way we look at them.

The Lasting Benefits of Good Service

If you feel you're being held back in life or that you're not getting enough of the things you should, to paraphrase the late John F. Kennedy, ask not what you can get but what you can do—what you can contribute to the causes and people it is given you to serve. Your rewards, believe me, will always take care of themselves.

Back in the year 1690, over three centuries ago, a wise gentleman by the name of John Locke wrote an essay on human understanding. In that essay, he said something I think all of us should remember:

"There seems to be a constant decay of all our ideas, even of those which are struck deepest, and in minds the most retentive; so that if they be not sometimes renewed, by repeated exercises of the senses, or reflection on those kinds of objects which at first occasioned them, the print wears out, and at last there remains nothing to be seen."

He was saying that we need reminding, from time to time, of our personal philosophies, of the things in which we believe and which mean so much to us in living successfully. If we're not reminded, we tend to forget, and gradually these truths, on which a successful life can be built, fade out until finally they disappear completely.

You can compare a human life to a plot of land—the yard in front of your home. Anyone can tell by looking at the front yard how much attention it's being given. There is no such thing as a poor-looking yard that's getting a lot of care and attention. Similarly, there is not, in all the world, a bad-looking plot of ground that's getting a lot of care and attention. If we take an average, sort of lackadaisical attitude toward our grounds, they'll reflect exactly that—and never get a second glance from anyone passing by.

It's the same thing with life. We'll get back—we must get back—exactly what we put into it—no more, no less. If we don't like the rewards we're receiving, we should examine our service, our contribution.

Now, I'm sure everyone will agree with this paraphrasing of the Golden Rule, when you remind them of it! But how about in between times? Isn't it a fact that even after we're forcibly brought to see this wonderful opportunity to get just about anything we want from life, it gradually begins to fade from our consciousness?

I think it's a very good idea for every human being to ask himself, "What am I contributing to those with whom I come in contact? Am I giving all that I can—am I doing as much as I can—and in a cheerful, helpful spirit? Or am I going at my daily life in an average, or even below average, manner?"

If you're tremendously pleased with the results you're getting from life, you're giving a lot. If you're not too pleased, well, you might think about it.

Every great law of life, like a coin, has two sides. If we work with these laws, we'll reap the benefits and rewards; if we try to work contrary to them, it will be to our cost—we cannot win.

YOUR GREATEST ASSET

Examine the rewards you are receiving in life. Are you giving as much as you could?

When was the last time you felt like you were stalled? Do you know why? Did you stop contributing?

Give to Get Rich

HERE ARE A FEW THOUGHTS that you can make your own thoughts, if you do make them your own, that will guarantee success all the years of your life. Now, that's quite a statement, but it's true.

To begin, let us understand that growth and increase are a part of mankind and all of nature. It is inherent in each of us to desire more. This is not wrong; it's perfectly natural and the way it should be. This is true of all of us—the members of our families, our friends and associates, our customers. You should want to get rich in every area of your life. But what do I mean by "rich"?

Getting rich, for you, is getting what you want very much. It may mean obtaining more love, greater peace of mind, owning the home of your dreams, or accomplishing something else you've set your heart upon. For some, it means a bigger income or a large sum of capital. That's fine. You can get it without hurting, or even competing with, any other person. In fact, you can thereby increase the general well-being of everyone with whom you come in contact.

Unfortunately, the uninformed believe that you can get ahead in the world only at the expense of someone else. This is not true. No one can become rich in any way without serving others. Anyone who adds to prosperity must prosper in turn.

The first step is to understand completely that it's right for you to want what you want. All human activities are based on the desire for increase—people seeking more food, more clothes, more knowledge, more pleasure, more life.

The next step is to understand that you need not compete with or deprive anyone. Don't compete. Create! In this way, you add to the general well-being without taking anything away from anyone.

Remember to give every person more than you take from him. Now, at first, this may sound absurd, so let's dig into it a little. In order for a business or a person to expand—and remember, expansion is the natural desire of mankind—we must give more in "use value" than we charge. A building nail doesn't cost much; yet its use is great and goes on for years. This book didn't cost much; yet if you can get ideas from it that can bring you more than you now have, it's use value will greatly exceed its cost.

How much does it cost to give love, respect, and consideration to those near you? Very little—just a little extra effort. Yet love, respect, and consideration are priceless to the person receiving them. This is the key: give more than you receive in everything you do. In this way, you are building a great credit for yourself that must come to you in some form, sooner or later. You are taking out less than you are putting in, and by so doing you are building a tidal wave of future prosperity. This is the law of increase. It is understood and followed undeviatingly by every successful business person, artist, professional, and worker; by every successful mother and father and friend. It is the most striking attribute of all successful people, companies, and institutions.

Now, let's go back to the idea of creating instead of competing. You are the point from which all increase must stem—not your company, your spouse, your parents or your friends. You are the creative center of your universe. Increase must come from you personally. Find ways to do the things you do that reflect you and your own unique talents and abilities. If you do this, no other person in the world can operate exactly as you do. You will not be competing with anyone; you will be creating from within yourself.

As you find new and better ways of giving more in use value than you are receiving in money, more and more people will turn to you. You will find your circle of friends increasing. If you are in business, you will find it continually growing, expanding. Do this in a quiet and unobtrusive manner. You don't have to shout about how much you are doing for others; they will recognize it and be drawn to you.

One of the most interesting things about such increase is that totally unexpected and wonderful things will begin to occur in your life. People you don't know, who have exactly what you need, will make their appearance at the right time and in the right place. Everything will begin to dovetail, and your life will take on new meaning and direction and bring you far greater rewards. Let the impression of growth, of increase, mark everything you do.

As you do these things, keep constantly before you the vision of what it is you intend to accomplish. Don't worry about it; don't fret about it. Just know you are going to accomplish it. And following these rules, you can't fail.

The Importance of Remaining Grateful

More than any other factor, gratitude projects the kind of picture that is irresistible. It attracts men, women, dogs, and cats. It also attracts a condition mistakenly known as "good luck."

HAVE YOU EVER NOTICED that when someone calls you on the telephone, you immediately form a mental picture of the person? You get not only a mental picture of his face and figure but also a feeling with regard to his personality. And that feeling you get is either good or bad. That is, the person affects you either pleasantly or unpleasantly. Your feelings are hardly ever neutral. They are either favorable or unfavorable.

And to carry it a step further, you project a picture in the minds of the people with whom you come in contact. And again, whether it's on the telephone or in person, that picture is either favorable or unfavorable.

You're projecting these pictures all day long to your children, your marriage partner, the people who serve you, your associates, your boss—everyone—all day, every day. So, how's your picture?

How do you appear to people passing by on the street? Do you appear happy? Unhappy? Bored? Disinterested? Worried? Successful? Or unsuccessful?

The picture you project, the way in which you communicate to every person with whom you come in contact during the day, is a reflection of your total personality; the picture you project is determined by how you feel inside.

The people who project the best pictures are those who know how to be grateful. Their gratitude for what they have, for what they are, radiates about them. They don't worry about what's missing but are grateful for what's there. They don't concentrate on the shortcomings of their marriage partner or their children; they're grateful just to have them. They look upon problems as things to be solved and are grateful for the capacity and wisdom to overcome them. These are the people who run deep.

More than any other factor, gratitude projects the kind of picture that's irresistible. It attracts men, women, dogs, and cats. It also attracts a condition mistakenly called "good luck."

These people are easy to recognize. There's a calm, level look to their eyes, and smiling comes as naturally to them as breathing does. They don't complain about what's to be done; they simply do it and do it well and then start looking around for something else to do. They radiate ability and good cheer like an old-fashioned stove radiates heat on a cold morning. They project a great picture, and the world projects it back to them.

Every minute of every waking hour of every day of your life, you're projecting a picture of yourself and your personality. You can tell how it looks to the world by looking at what you're getting back.

A Personal Creation of Value

ONE OF THE TRULY GREAT THINGS that accrued to the old-time craftsman and to the few still remaining was the joy that came from the meaning of doing, the feeling of value that pervades a person's whole being when she does something of which she's proud. This feeling is found in the person who knits or does needlepoint, the painter, the writer, the cabinet maker, the really good cook, the workman or woman who creates something of value. And I think that's where it comes from—the personal creation of value.

Do you know what I mean? If you do, you know that it's a large part of a person's income—his psychic income, so important to living and good healthy adjustment. The distinguished social critic, Louis Mumford, has written that "the fact is that with all our superabundance of energy, food, materials, products, there has been no commensurate improvement in the quality of our daily existence."

He said, "The great mass of comfortable, well-fed people in our civilization live lives of emotional apathy and mental torpor, of dull passivity and enviable desire, lives that belie the real potentialities of modern culture." He's also pointed out that the fault lies in forcing something that is capable of producing goods in great numbers to provide more and more, more on top of more, more every month, every year, until quality and beauty must be destroyed in the process, until there's so much that we no longer appreciate.

Mumford's concern—and I think every thinking person will agree with his concern—is with balance and self-discipline, with the sort of person who will do intelligently and well whatever he turns his hand to because he understands the meaning of doing, the meaning of value—not only in that to which he turns his hand, but in his life as well.

There's meaning in doing something well—anything, really. You know, there are no so-called "good jobs" and "bad jobs." Every job holds within it the road to greatness if it's done well. And it can give us the meaning and satisfaction that come from doing a job as well as we can learn to do it. It's wonderful these days when we find a person who does an unusually good job—a waitress; a service station attendant; a mechanic; a salesperson; a carpenter, plumber, or other craftsman; an attorney, doctor, whomever. We run into them from time to time, and we never fail to notice and be aware of them. Such people always seem happier, more cheerful, and have a much better self-image. They seem to find joy and delight in their work, in their days. And they seem to understand that there is meaning in doing, in doing what they do as well as they can. They take a few extra pains that converts what would otherwise be an ordinary job into something special. They stand out like a fresh oasis in the dismal desert of uninteresting sameness, and they realize that the meaning they find in doing brings meaning into their lives. They're happier people because of it. You know them. Perhaps you're one of them. If so, congratulations. You're the member of an exclusive club.

> ## YOUR GREATEST ASSET
>
> **Do you find meaning in the job you do?**
>
> **Are you happy during your workday?**
>
> **How does this reflect how you feel about the work you do?**
>
> **Is it time to make a change?**

The Art of Excellence

JAMES B. CONANT, when he was president of Harvard University, commented, "Each honest calling, each walk of life, has its own elite, its own aristocracy, based upon excellence of performance." Beautiful. People in every field of human endeavor will agree with that remark.

Aristotle said, "Excellence is an art won by training and habituation. We do not act rightly because we have virtue or excellence, but we rather have those because we have acted rightly. We are what we repeatedly do. Excellence, then, is not an act but a habit."

By judging the excellence (or the lack of it) of our work, we can tell if we're in the right calling. If it's of paramount importance to us to strive for excellence in what we do, chances are we're in the kind of work for which we're best fitted, or, at least, one of the fields for which we're qualified.

One of the problems of the businessperson is that after developing and profiting from a few good ideas, he will tend to stay with it in unchanging form for too long. For some things, that will work; but for most things, it won't. They need updating on a regular, annual basis. We need to ask ourselves at regular intervals a number of times each year, "How can we make it better, more efficient? How can we bring it up to the best of present—even future—standards?"

People will cling to an idea as though it's the best, if not the only, idea they'll ever get. And when we're creating or building something, are we anticipating the future? A good example of foresight is found in the main streets of towns and cities built by the Mormons when they moved west. They were riding horses and driving wagons

The Lasting Benefits of Good Service

then, but they built broad, beautiful streets that easily accommodate the heavy automobile traffic of today.

We tend to cling too long to past successes, systems, and methods. If it's working well today, look at it with the future in mind. We're seeing an accelerated rate of change unprecedented in history. And because so many businesses are still living in the past, there are yawning opportunities on practically every side.

How many businesses in your town haven't made a single change in twenty years? In some cases, that may work—for example, a fine old restaurant that is perhaps now, more than ever, excellent because of its age and strict adherence to quality. But the businesspeople of a community owe it to their customers and the community to keep abreast of excellence, to put part of their profits back into the business to accommodate changing times and tastes.

As James B. Conant said, "Each honest calling, each walk of life, has its own elite, its own aristocracy, based upon excellence of performance." That applies to every field of human endeavor.

We can develop habits of excellence in everything we do. We need to think in terms of excellence. We should demand it in what we buy and produce and in what we do.

Don't Do Something New; Do Something Better

To become successful and outstanding at something, we don't have to come up with something new; we need only find ways of doing it better.

A FRIEND OF MIND passed along to me an old, out-of-print book entitled The Magic of a Name. It's about the beginnings of the Rolls Royce automobile, written by Harold Nockolds and first published in 1938. It makes for interesting reading. But the point that underlies the story is the fact that the originator of the Rolls Royce automobile, Henry Royce, was an indefatigable perfectionist. He didn't invent the automobile; he just wasn't happy with it. He thought it was too noisy, for one thing, and too heavy and inefficient.

And so it happened that in Manchester, England, on April 1, 1904, there came into being a motorcar unlike any other that had been seen or heard before. As Harold Nockolds put it, "Save for a gentle phut-phut, phut-phut from its exhaust pipe, it made no noise at all. There was no clatter from the engine, no grinding from the gears and back axle; and this comparative silence, in the days when the noise of a motorcar had been likened with deadly accuracy to 'an avalanche of tea trays,' was something indeed to marvel at."

"At the wheel of this miraculous machine sat a bearded figure of some forty years of age, whose piercing eyes were lit with a gleam

The Lasting Benefits of Good Service

of triumphant concentration." It was Henry Royce, later called Sir Henry, the perfectionist.

The trade name of Rolls Royce went on to become synonymous with anything excellent or outstanding. The Spitfires in the Battle of Britain in 1940, which had Rolls Royce engines, were a big factor in winning that war. In fact, there's a beautiful stained-glass memorial window at the Rolls Royce aircraft engine plant commemorating the pilots of the Royal Air Force, and it reads: "...who, in the Battle of Britain, turned the work of our hands into the salvation of our country."

But the point I want to make is that to become successful and outstanding at something, we don't have to come up with something new; we need only find ways of doing it better. If you'll think about it, it's the key element in virtually all success stories: Hilton Hotels, Holiday Inns, Kentucky Fried Chicken, McDonald's hamburgers—the list is endless. If you want to succeed at something, just do it better.

Henry Royce was so wrapped up in the business of producing a superior automobile, he would forget to eat for days at a time and sleep on a bench in the foundry. A boy was hired to follow him around with a glass of milk and some bread so he wouldn't get sick from malnutrition.

He once heard a mechanic make the statement, "OK, that's good enough!" and they almost had to tie Royce down. Nothing was good enough for him, and his name and the name of his salesman-distributor-partner, C. S. Rolls, is a symbol of quality.

It's the same in every field—from advertising to zinnia growing. Give it the kind of study and all-out dedication that Royce gave to his cars, and your name will someday stand like some of those I listed earlier.

I remember reading a few years ago about a Canadian farmer who sold his Stradivarius violin for, I think, somewhere in the neighborhood of $460,000. They're worth much more than that now. He sold it back to the same New York City dealer he'd bought it from many years before, and for the same price. The farmer sold his precious violin by the world's most famous violin craftsman because, as he put it, "I'm getting old, and I have no children to leave it to." By getting it back into the hands of the dealer, he knew that it would get into the hands of someone who would treasure it as he had.

Antonio Stradivari, the Italian violinmaker, lived from 1644 to 1737. That's 93 years—a remarkable lifespan at a time when the average life expectancy was perhaps about thirty. He lived for his work, and his work has lived on ever since. He worked alone, although later in life his sons helped him. His tools were rather primitive by our standards, but that was not important. He put himself and his genius into his work, and his instruments sang with a power and poignancy—a purity that, in the hands of fine violinists, delighted all who heard them.

When he was finished with an instrument and he was sure that it was up to his personal standards, he signed his name to it. And still today, nearly 250 years later, his name is famous the world over, and his fine instruments still are delighting millions.

Throughout history, there have been many with similar standards of excellence in many fields—artists such as William Shakespeare and Leonardo da Vinci, craftsmen such as furniture maker Thomas Chippendale and silversmith Paul Revere. Everything they did was done exceptionally well—not because there was any pressure other than their own insistence on excellence beyond the reach of others of their time.

A good violinist can give you the names of other violin makers who are great and whose instruments are cherished, and it's the same in all fields. There are many thousands of craftsmen and women who will not turn out shoddy or even ordinary work and would be glad to sign their names to their work.

The respect for excellence never changes. It still commands the highest price; it is still revered wherever we find it. And the people performing the work have gained for themselves two precious assets: (1) They have gained the kind of security that lasts a lifetime, of course. They never need worry about income. There is always a ready market for the best. And (2) their work is a source of satisfaction and joy to them. They derive deep satisfaction from being uncommon people turning out uncommonly fine products or services.

Would you be willing to sign your name to what you do? I think most of us would. Our work, after all, is a kind of mirror of ourselves.

Earl Nightingale's Biography

AS A DEPRESSION-ERA CHILD, Earl Nightingale was hungry for knowledge. From the time he was a young boy, he would frequent the Long Beach Public Library in New York, searching for the answer to the question, "How can a person, starting from scratch, who has no particular advantage in the world, reach the goals that he feels are important to him, and by so doing, make a major contribution to others?" His desire to find an answer, coupled with his natural curiosity about the world and its workings, spurred him to become one of the world's foremost experts on success and what makes people successful.

His early career began when, as a member of the Marine Corps, he volunteered to work at a local radio station as an announcer, sharing some of the ideas he had uncovered during his inquisitive youth. The Marines also give him his first chance to travel, although he only got as far as Hawaii when the Japanese attacked Pearl Harbor in 1941. Earl managed to be one of the few survivors aboard the battleship *Arizona*. After five more years in the service, Earl and his wife moved first to Phoenix, then to Chicago, to build what was to be a very fruitful career in network radio. As the host of his own daily commentary program on WGN, Earl arranged a deal that also gave him a commission on his own advertising sales. By 1957, he was so successful he decided to retire at the age of thirty-five.

In the meantime, he had bought his own insurance company and had spent many hours motivating its sales force to greater profits. When he decided to go on vacation for an extended period of time, his sales manager begged him to put his inspirational words on record. The result later became the recording entitled *The Strangest Secret*, the first spoken word message to win a Gold Record by selling over a million copies. About this time, Earl met a successful businessman by the name of Lloyd Conant, and together they began an electronic publishing company that eventually grew to become a multimillion-dollar giant in the self-improvement field. They also developed a syndicated, five-minute, daily radio program, *Our Changing World*, which became the longest-running, most widely syndicated show in radio. Nightingale-Conant Corporation has gone on to publish the audiocassette programs of such well-known authors as Tom Peters, Harvey Mackay, Napoleon Hill, Leo Buscaglia, Denis Waitley, Roger Dawson, Wayne Dyer, Brian Tracy, Tony Robbins, and others too numerous to mention—all leaders in personal and professional development.

When Earl Nightingale died on March 28, 1989, Paul Harvey broke the news to the country on his radio program with the words,

"The sonorous voice of the nightingale was stilled." While he was alive, Earl had found an answer to the question that had inspired him as a youth. He was able to reach valuable goals and, in turn, leave a lasting legacy for others. He had created a life that defines what it means to be "The Essence of Success." In the words of his good friend and commercial announcer Steve King, "Earl Nightingale never let a day go by that he didn't learn something new and, in turn, to pass it on to others. It was his consuming passion."

To claim your additional free resources, please visit
soundwisdom.com/nightingale-conant-books

OFFICIAL PUBLICATIONS OF
Nightingale Conant

Get Your Copy Today!

Available Everywhere Books Are Sold

Lead the Field   Your Success Starts Here   Transformational Living
The Direct Line   The Direct Line Action Guide

sound wisdom
www.soundwisdom.com